Gray Matters

Brain Injury:
The Inside Perspective

Heidi Lerner, M.A.

Bloomington, IN  Milton Keynes, UK

AuthorHouse™
1663 Liberty Drive, Suite 200
Bloomington, IN 47403
www.authorhouse.com
Phone: 1-800-839-8640

AuthorHouse™ UK Ltd.
500 Avebury Boulevard
Central Milton Keynes, MK9 2BE
www.authorhouse.co.uk
Phone: 08001974150

© 2006 Heidi Lerner. All rights reserved.

No part of this book may be reproduced, stored in a retrieval system, or transmitted by any means without the written permission of the author.

First published by AuthorHouse 8/29/2006

ISBN: 1-4259-2970-2 (sc)
ISBN: 1-4259-2971-0 (dj)

Library of Congress Control Number: 2006904418

Printed in the United States of America
Bloomington, Indiana

This book is printed on acid-free paper.

Where are the dreams that we once had?
This is the time to bring them back.
Where are the promises we've made to ourselves?
They're caught on the tips of our tongue -

How long must we all want to change
Our world bound in chains?
You say you're aware and that you care, but...
Do you care enough?
Where's your conviction of the heart?

"We're one with the earth and the sky,
One with everything alive...
One child, one dream,
There's only one chance,

I believe,
It will start,
With conviction of the heart!"

(Kenny Loggins, 1991)

Dedication

This book is dedicated to each and every person (child, adult or senior citizen) who has sustained a brain injury and confronts the every day challenges of survival. I seek to educate the public about brain injury, and I do this for you. We all need to be understood! I toast each of you for your inner strength, adaptability and persistence.

Additionally, I dedicate this book to my uncle, T.J. and my dear friend, Lillian.

It's a Good Life

Everything was fine,
Then one day
My life buckled under.
Now I walk around,
My scars are under cover,

I swam up and jumped aboard again.
Sure, there are some functional irregularities,
But I'm glad to have another time around the bend.

This is a "Cheers" to those that trauma has taken for a fall,
For we all agree that it's a good life, after all!

Acknowledgements

I give special appreciation to:

- All of those who have helped me through my rehab and schooling, as well as those who have helped me to get by day to day, with my personal challenges.

- My family - for no matter what the circumstances, always being able to resort to a smile and some laughter. This has been my saving grace.

- The community of folks with brain injury - they have been my reflection and inspiration, and have helped to bring forth some needed laughter as well as a reminder to keep smiling. They showed me that what I carry on the inside is contagious!

- Lastly, I want to thank the Lord for gifting me with the inspiration, motivation and talent to speak my mind and heart through my poetry.

Personal Story

Heidi Lerner was in a severe car wreck on October 25th, 1989 (i.e. her mother's birthday). She was traveling a long distance and fell asleep at the wheel. She drifted off to the right side of the road, her car tumbled and she went flying through the windshield for about 50 feet. She sustained a Traumatic Brain Injury and went into an immediate comatose state. A man passing by on the highway discovered her and called 911. She was carried off to the nearest trauma hospital by an emergency helicopter. Her family was notified and immediately came to her bedside. Heidi remained in a coma for nine days.

Upon awakening, she did not recognize her parents. After a couple of weeks in the hospital, she figured that they must be her parents, they'd been there for long enough! Her parents still joke with her about this. Heidi, who additionally had fractured her left clavicle and also sustained significant dental trauma, remained in intensive care at University of Mississippi Medical Center, for approximately 3 1/2 weeks.

Continuing on in rehab, she was transferred to the brain injury program at Brynn Mar Rehabilitation Hospital in Malvern, Pennsylvania, where she spent 3-4 weeks in the secured ward of the Inpatient Rehab (There, Heidi and her roommate would pass time strategizing about how they would break out of their hospital cell!). After release from the hospital, she then accompanied her parents in their residence in South Florida; it was there she participated in The Palm House Consortium for Rehabilitation's Outpatient Life Skills Program for 3-4 months.

Soon after this, Heidi moved back into her pre-injury living situation. The only thing was Heidi was not the same as she had been before the accident. Nevertheless, she saw to it that she got by ok, despite all the changes. She had worked with people with disabilities before her injury and though not capable of employment at the time, her interests in this field grew.

Six years after her injury, Heidi decided that she wanted to help people with disabilities better care for themselves. She decided to pursue her Masters in Special Education. She discovered that George Washington University had a scholarship program in Special Education and that it was the only university in the entire country at that time with a graduate program specifically designed to teach Special Education to survivors of Traumatic Brain Injury. Heidi applied and to her surprise, was accepted. Washington DC was close to her hometown, so Heidi moved back home to start on the rugged path of going for her Masters degree. Attending George Washington University was a struggle for her. Many wondered if she would make it. Heidi wondered if she would make it. With support from her family, she remained motivated and achieved her academic goal.

While in school, Heidi was awarded a government sponsored research grant to investigate how best to educate survivors of brain injury. Her inner glimpse led her to discern the need for research into the internal workings of brain injury, and she targeted the role of personal motivation in the rehabilitation from traumatic brain injury (For a synopsis of the research, see http://www.graymatters4u.com). The main research question approached was: Will students participate more actively in rehabilitation if the therapy incorporates their interests? Interventions led to increased self-confidence and incredible leaps in ability.

Heidi's other endeavors in the field of brain injury include the designing and facilitating of brain injury support groups. She conducts a brain injury support group under the name of Gray Matters at Scripps Hospital, in Southern California. Heidi has a proactive approach that engages all of the participants. She creates a safe space where people feel welcome to share burdens, blessings or just the blah-ness of life. She encourages constructive input and a spirit of fun-loving support. Everyone leaves the meeting feeling good and looking forward to further group interactions.

At the time of this book's publishing, it was 16 years since Heidi's injury. She has continued her development with becoming a trainer in Pilates rehabilitative exercise. Her specialty in Pilates lays in working with Senior Citizens and people with special needs. Heidi has a holistic approach; depending on the client's individual needs, she is prepared to help a person cognitively, emotionally, psycho-socially, physically, as well as with life skills. She feels competent in helping others with individualized needs and concerns, because she has learned how to adapt and compensate in her own inner healing.

Heidi now lives in Southern California. She is happiest living close to the ocean as this is where she finds the greatest peace of mind and creative inspiration, as well as time for surf kayaking.

Table of Contents

Dedication vi
   It's a Good Life vii
Foreword .... x-xi
Introduction 1

Brain Injury 6

   Silent Epidemic 7
      It's spreading 7
      The Virus 9
      Anti-bacterial 11
   Disclosure 14
   Trauma's Unceasing Harvest 16
   Enigma 18
   Change 21
   Trauma 22
   Coma 25
   Near Death 27
   Broken Wings 29
   Lost in Thought 31
   Scramble 32
   Paved Paradise 33

Sequelae 40

   Post Traumatic Stress 42
   Memory 44
   Attending 46
   Mood Swing 48
   Psychosociality 51
   Melt Down 53
   Impulsivity 56

Self-Importance 58
Anger Management 60
The O Word 61
Aphasia 63
Light Sensitivity 65
Anti-Depressed 66
Inhibition 69
Moe 71

Rehabilitation 76

Celebration 79
Metacognitive 81
The Unpaved Road 83
Survivor 86
Invisible Disability 88
Peer Counselor 90
Visioning 92
Inner Cave 96
Riding on G-d's Plan 98
Closure 100
Healing 102
"Disabled" 106
Rehabilitative Exercise 108
Life Moves 111
Keeping the Faith 116

The Brain 120

Master Organ 122
Neuron 126
Frontal Lobe 128
Limbic System 129
Left Hemisphere 130
Right Hemisphere 131
The Balance of the Poet 132

Academia 136

Academic Arena 138
Special Education for Brain Injury 141
Environment 143
Directing Traffic 145
Can Creativity Enhance Cognition? 148

Nature's Touch 154

Land Lovers – Imagine This 155
Ocean Manna 159
sea of translucence 160
Maggie 163
Kayak Trip Report 166
Nature Heals 169
Interspecies Communication 172
Shared Adventure 173
Eskimo roll 179
Surf Sense 180
No Sound Barriers 183
Consider This 185

Circle of Support 190

Josephine 192
Mirrors 197
Type of Injury 199
What Survivors Want in a Support Group 200
Greatest Challenge 203
Greatest Advantage of Having a Head Injury ... 205
What Can Help a Brain Injury Survivor? 207

Glossary	211
Appendix	219
Bibliography	234
Musical References	236
Online References	237
Endnotes	239

She will share her word with those who will,
Take the time and drink their fill,
She's lot of message in her verb,
We will keep quiet,
For now is her turn.

(Anonymous, 2003)

Heidi Lerner

Poet and He Don't Know It

Foreword

This inspiring book of poetry by Heidi Lerner offers readers an opportunity to experience the shattered and confusing world of recovery from a traumatic brain injury through the perspective of someone who has been there. Research has shown that approximately 5.3 million people in our country live with the effects of an injury to their brain, and over 30,000 children and youth are disabled from brain injury each year[i] - but these are only statistics. It is the individual person's unique experience and recovery from brain injury that we need to better understand. Brain injury can happen to you, me, or anyone we know at a moment's notice; life is forever changed for that person and those connected to him or her.

Aldous Huxley said, "experience is not what happens to you, it is what you do with what happens to you" (Texts and Pretexts, 1933). In writing this book of profound and sensitive poetry, Ms. Lerner has used her own traumatic experience to help others. She shows us the process that a survivor of brain injury goes through in using disoriented and confused thinking to figure out the world again. She shows us the complexities of brain injury recovery through the language of poetry that helps us to feel brain injury rather than merely observe it or study it as a professionally interesting "subject".

Cognitive disability resulting from a brain injury is often described as a hidden disability, because most people do not fully understand the vast scope of cognition. All too often, we ignore what is right in front of us. A little girl struggling to keep up in school; a lonely teenager who just can't connect with his friends anymore; or an unemployed man or woman who has lost another job because no one explained how to do some things he used to know how to do (for neither s/he nor the boss recognized s/he had lost that knowledge or skill). These are the day-to-day problems that people with brain injuries live with that so few people fully understand and have adequate training to help.

Ms. Lerner's book will no doubt raise public awareness about the thoughts, feelings, and needs of someone with a brain injury, as well as the need for increased support and education regarding this disability. Readers will enjoy a book of beautiful poetry that demonstrates that after a brain injury, a person is not only still able to function, but is able to live, reflect, write, and give meaning to the experience for others.

Janis Ruoff, PhD – Special Education Administration, Director, Center for Education and Human Services in Acquired Brain Injury, George Washington University.

Introduction

Purpose

The goal of Gray Matters is to specially educate about brain injury and it's complications. The target audience of this book is twofold. The primary aim is being a support – intellectually, psychologically, and emotionally for those who have sustained a brain injury. The secondary purpose is to educate the public about what it feels like to have a brain injury. In other words, I want you to know what it's like to walk in my shoes!

Many people can't even begin to imagine what a brain injury is like. Oftentimes, when I disclose about my injury, I get a blank stare. I get the impression that I'm speaking a whole other reality to the people who give me these vacant looks. Well, it is a mountain to climb, but it is my goal to try and educate these people, and the public in general. In my writing and in my rhyme, I work silently (but with a loud pen) to minimize ignorance about brain injury by developing comprehension and understanding. I aim to increase awareness of brain injury for survivors, families and friends, professionals in the field of rehabilitation as well as the generally interested public.

Wake Up Call

Please try and understand that people with brain injury do not lose their intelligence. What happens is that a survivor's functions just get tied up in knots. Everyone has their different areas of entanglement. I am imagining a person speaking slow and simple to a person with a brain injury (in the acute phase, for some, this may be appropriate), but s/he cannot project that need onto another brain injury survivor, as that may seem idiotic, or even belittling. A sensitivity to individual needs and abilities is what is necessary to acknowledge personal challenges for a person who has survived a head injury.

Terri Schiavo had quite a severe brain injury. Not so many cases are as severe as hers; quite a lot of people have had minor head injuries that haven't had it reported and can't even recognize the symptoms. Nevertheless, statistics state that just a little more than 2% of the US population (approximately 5.3 million), currently live with a Traumatic Brain Injury (TBI-see Glossary). One and a half million Americans are reported to sustain a Traumatic Brain Injury each year.[i] So many people in this country suffer from TBI, and we have no way of identifying who these survivors may be! I ask - what is it like to function in this world with a less debilitating brain injury than Terry Schiavo? How can survivors of brain injury be recognized and attended to? I believe that Terri Schiavo would have wanted people to understand the complications of the disability, rather than count survivors unacceptable because of their differences.

Traumatic Brain Injury is termed by some professionals, as the Silent Epidemic. I think it is silent largely because we are unaware of what TBI entails. It is similar with ADD; decades ago, not many knew about the syndrome, so people just thought they were spacey or something of the like. How many of us have been knocked on the head, even went unconscious, and after the pain went away, forgot about it? Additionally, many are not fully aware of the full range of cognitive, emotional or psychosocial skills that may be affected by an injury to the brain. For these reasons, the symptoms of brain injury are rarely recognized. Usually what happens is a person winds up blaming him or herself for being stupid. I believe it is time for us to stand up, swallow and digest some good, down home understanding of the complexities of brain injury.

Evolution

In this technologically advanced age, isn't it a shame that we are so unfamiliar with our own master organ, the brain? It is time to consciously step over our stumbling stones in order to allow for greater advances in consciousness. As the monkeys showed us in the Hundredth Monkey,[ii] there is a point at which if only one more person (the 100th) becomes more aware, the field of consciousness is strengthened so that the majority picks up this awareness! Perhaps I am visioning the hundredth person starting to "wash their sweet potatoes before eating them" or becoming more conscientious of brain injury. This will then cause a great leap in consciousness for all. The world will become a better place for people recovering from and surviving head trauma; it will develop into a place where people will exhibit greater understanding and tolerance.

Diffuse

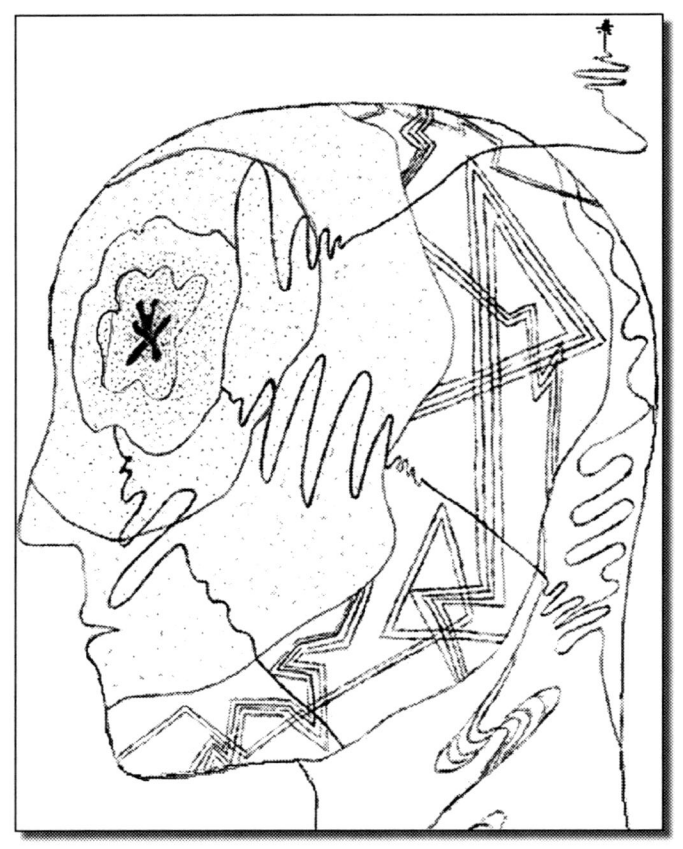

Heidi Lerner

Brain Injury

- Silent Epidemic
  - It's Spreading
  - The Virus
  - Anti-Bacterial
- Disclosure
- Trauma's Unceasing Harvest
- Enigma
- Change
- Trauma
- Coma
- Near Death
- Broken Wings
- Lost in Thought
- Scramble
- Paved Paradise

Brain Injury

Looking across the broad expanse of sky, feeling the vastness of space and the magnificence of the stars, I pick up a pen and try to describe my perception. I am stultified by the comprehensiveness. I resist writing in fear of not being able to capture it all. Brain injury is as vast as the night's sky! I take a full breath; the journey of articulation starts with picking up my pen. Challenges present themselves for our personal growth. I blow truth into the ink of my expression.

My aim is not just to tell my personal story, although I do perspire beads of myself throughout my writing. Most books about brain injury do just that, tell the author's personal story. I desire something greater for my readers; I want my readers to come away with a depth of appreciation for what it is like to walk in the shoes of a brain injury survivor. I most often use myself as an example - because to have any clout, it's me I'm only qualified to talk about! For the sake of my readers' curiosity, at the beginning of the book, I did briefly describe my own personal saga.

It is important that you understand the resources at stake:

I don't just speak from experiential psychology,
Or my own cerebral topography,
It's not merely verbal photography,
There's research behind it,
Just check the bibliography!

Silent Epidemic

It's spreading

Traumas perpetually occur.
Every 21 seconds,
One person in the US
Sustains a Traumatic Brain Injury.
These are the statistics,
This is what continually happens,
Of this we can be assured,
We are now just coming to know,
What we have already incurred.

Brain injury isn't new,
Cave woman club man over head,
Back then,
You think it turned into something else instead?

Silenced,
Moving like a slug through time,
Brain injury then,
Brain injury now,
Epidemic...
Silently carrying on the infection somehow.

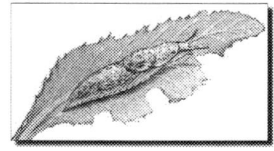

Do you think ADD did not exist 20 years ago?
Before the research...
It just wasn't explored,
Now, it is quite prevalent,
Yet it is not new,
It's a silent reality,
Until it affects you!

Why is brain injury soundless?
Car crashes are not quiet,
Yet the injury is reported to be silent,
Quieter than a whisper,
Why?
Perhaps...
Maybe...

Mystery lays in the unknown -
Thoughts make noise,
Ignorance is quiet,
People aren't aware,
Silence isn't the epidemic,
The hush covers -
Allows for infectious growth,
It spreads in a cloud of mystery...

Brain injury can even be invisible,
Folks can't see it,
Haven't heard about it,
Unblemished minds think...
What would it be without me?
What exactly is brain injury?

The Virus [iii]

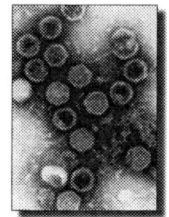

We can trace symptoms
in several areas:
Cognitive, Emotional,
Psycho-social, Behavioral.
We've got to be careful
when we categorize,
...We don't always see things
through holistic eyes.

One category rebounds
off of the other,
Sometimes they blend,
Then it's hard to tell one from another.
Scientists cut away to observe
one function with proficience,
But this profoundly takes away
from the personal experience.
For science,
They're trying to observe the facts,
But in real life,
It just doesn't happen like that!

My crowned-prince
Endured the epidemic.
For him, some think it's just academic.
Sometimes he doesn't feel he fits his role,
I encourage him,
To help him get more in control.
I give him regal countenance,
He's the captain of my ship.
He takes me for a ride,
And connects me
With the Silent One inside.

We work together as a team,
I try to feed his confidence,
Encourage his self-esteem.
If his motivation sinks to the ground floor,
I give positive feedback
Help him up,
Then watch him soar!

Anti-bacterial

For a brain injury survivor,
The epidemic is far from quiet,
It is –
Pervasive,
Comprehensive,
Undeniable,

Life gets off skew,
GOT TO GET A BALANCE!
Organic dysfunction,
24-7... dealing!
Rehabilitation is a full time job.

Survivors want to scream from the hilltops!
Sing it to the masses,
Break the curse of silence!
No one wants to be denied,
We certainly don't want to hide!

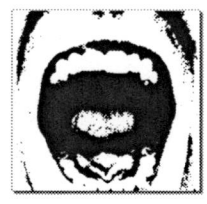

You need to know on the inside,
What it's like to walk in my shoes,
I'm going to telepathically communicate it,
I need to,
I said it is my need
To communicate this with you.

I'll take you on a fun trip,
Yes, and of brain injury
You'll be more hip,
I have the will,
I am committed,
Determined,
I light on fire
on the mission -

Gray Matters

The doors have been closed,
The mind and heart have yet to awaken,
We're inserting the key
to open the gates,
Enter and you can feel,
It's ok to care,

Because empathy heals.

I said IT'S OK TO CARE!
Melt those stones in there,
Love rebounds
When it's found.

Gray Matters

I'm calling to all around the nation,
Let us sing in chorus,
Break the silence,
Let's raise a ruckus,
Hip, hip hoorah,
Hip, hip hooray,
Together,
We'll draw a close
To the silent dismay.

This is a call to awareness -
I'm making a shout,
So the bacterial stain
We can clean out.

Pick up my book,
Listen to my rhyme,
I'll have you captivated in no time!
Pass on the word of what you hear,
We are breaking the silence,
Thanks to your receptive ear.
We're paving the way for knowledge,
We are the pioneers...

Gray Matters!

Disclosure

I am writing this just for you,
Because I intend to give you a clue,

My poetry comes from my own inner construct,
I give you markings so you can at least draw dot to dot,

I want to personally disclose this to you,
So you can better understand what I speak to,

I've been through some life experiences that do awaken -
Well, I've had my nagen shaken,

That is a Traumatic Brain Injury,
I want you to discern what it does to me.

Cerebral bruising, tearing, bleeding & swelling,
Not just mental impairments, there's much more to be telling,

I'll translate this into real life,
So you can understand my neurological strife.

I want you to better see,
So you can more competently talk with someone like me,

Perhaps for me it is quite healing,
For others to have more of this feeling,

I'm not going to play the cosmic trickster,
I want to point you to the holistic picture,

I will communicate what I can,
So people with brain injuries you can better understand.

I talk straight from the heart in my chatter,
I say this to you, because **GRAY MATTERS**!

Trauma's Unceasing Harvest

Have you heard anything
Regarding injury to the brain?
For in your heart,
You'd think it's such a shame.

Lets take Jimmy here,
He's a friend of mine.
Walking to school one day,
Everything was just fine,

Ready to cross the street,
Two cars hit with a CRASH!
One car rebounded,
And laid Jimmy in the grass.

Sent him right into dreamland,
Twenty days in a coma, or more,
Now he's battling with himself
Just to do every day chores.

He sees a therapist regularly,
The way he handles
I don't know how,
But let's ask Jimmy
How he's doing now.

"It was hard for me at first,
Everything seemed so strange.
Yet my teacher tells me,
That nothing's changed!

The girl that I used to like,
We'd meet out on the track
When our classes were free,
Now she won't even look at me!

To tell you the truth,
I don't know
If I want to be here in school,
They all look at me
Like I'm such a fool."

Well thank you Jimmy
For speaking your mind.
Just know that out there
Are people that care.
Them, I'm sure that you will find.

Being dragged through the wringer,
Jimmy starts his wrinkled life anew,
And as much as you may have heard,
Do you really know what Jimmy's going through?

Enigma

Puzzling,
Ambiguous,
Inexplicable,
I crack open the window,
To let in the light,
Yet I am usually suspended in the dark.
I am an enigma.

Saturated in deep, dark color,
Purples, Blues, Greens, Black,
The light seeps in through the cracks,
The Tree of Life germinates inside,
It grows in hidden places,
Aiming toward the light.

Life's movement continues on.
A spectrum of emotions
Dance themselves awake -
I am grateful,
Lonely,
Caring,
Hurt,
Loving,
Frustrated,
All welled up inside,
And I look to the sky with an eye of hope.

In storms of tears,
I feel the pain of the earth.
Most others don't give a damn -
Hypocrites!
They say one thing,
Yet mean another.
Stomping all over each other,
They march towards their success.
I want to hide,
Disintegrate into the earth,
Disappear,
Perhaps as an earthworm
In the compost heap.
- Don't step on me,
You hypocrites!

I see through your lies,
Can you not see them yourselves?
You cannot intrude into my life.
I protect myself
with a strong shield of truth.
Cerebral penetration
has created my own living hell,
Now I must walk my walk,
Talk my talk,
At least I walk my talk.

The Tree of Life grows strong branches inside,
It reaches out to the world,
Blooming new growths,
Regenerating me.
It's both certain and for sure,
The darkness is tightly woven in,
The dance of the light and the dark
Creates my enigma.

I bleed myself free.

Change

Always watching...
Is that appropriate?

Camouflage to fit the scenery,
Altering our behavior
To better suit the circumstance,

We know of you -
Who build your mountain
of unchanging rock.

Your stagnancy never knows
of its "inappropriateness".

You think you can stand tall and assured forever?
So strong -
In your rock solid way of being,

You'd better keep track of yourself,
You just may erode away.

...The waters flow on,
Streams contour the
mountainside,

Behavior is cultivated,
We need to be willing to adapt,
Be refined,

We sculpt ourselves complete,
Molded by the flow of change.

Trauma

Shock, disturbance, disbelief,
Impact, daze, stupor,

Daunting episode shocks the moment,
Numbness of feeling,
Amnesia beckons,
(Post-Traumatic Amnesia - see Glossary)

Horrendous incident,
Remembered only by the Eternal Mind.
Memories implanted subconsciously,
For me to later find.
(Post-Traumatic Stress – see Glossary)

Off for a journey into Dreamland,
Now under a Greater Hand,

Stability is shaken,
How I've known myself to be is taken.

Change - a variable that becomes a constant,
Rehab involves persistent modification,

Old habits are no longer my friends,
Things will never be the same again,

Devastation of myself,
Impairments have settled in...

In my spirit,
I must accept & allow,
In my body,
I must figure out how.

I must permit
that I now go at a slower pace,
In today's world,
It does help me -
to not always be moving in such a haste!

Processing slowed,
It takes so long
to get things done.
I try
to structure my time,
Set goals...
But it can be glorious,
When I actually
accomplish one!
(Hallelujah for the completion of this book!)

To the ordinary eye,
Everything seems just fine,
Yet I feel inner torment,
Pulling me from both sides
at the same time.

~~((*))~~

And here I am,
Radiant smile,
Alive
and shining!
Tolerant heart,
Changed from the outside in,

I take a breath of fresh air -
Saved...
From I don't know where!

Coma

spiritual rest
like never known
sleep?
eternal wakefulness

thrashing
the body never rests
in this world
but not of it
restless sleep

here
but somewhere else
visited
touched
someone is always looking out for us

end result
life
enduring faith
without question

i was in a coma
therefore i live

(Coma - see glossary)

Near Death

Oh, the uncertainties of life,
Catapulted into the tunnel,
Unexplored territories,
No end in sight.
I retreat back
To a child exploring nature -
Where does this lead to, anyway?

"You took a shock to your head,
But your Bubby's looking out for you."

She parted the sea
To come to me.
She pointed my way,
Because there I couldn't stay.
To walk that way I did dare,
But it was not my time to be there.

"Yea, though I walk,
Through the valley of the shadow of death,
I will fear no evil,
For thou art with me...
Surely goodness and mercy
Shall follow me all the days of my life,
And I will dwell in the house of the Lord,
Forever."[iv]

Back home again,
Complications have set in...
We all know that Cain slew Label,
Kindred wounds,
The heart disables.
Thorns and thistles,
Comfort,
Distress,
Good and evil,
Tree of knowledge.

The Lord's mercy reigns,
Though not as we may expect it.
As we go amidst the brush -
We must rely on the Lord,
Try to trust,
We've all got our own list of mistakes...
I just try and remember,
Forgiveness is good for our own sake.

Death is a very humbling thing to live with.

Broken Wings

Every day was stable,
Everything was so for sure,
Even between the lines,
Things were certain,
...Then one day I cracked my skull.
Praise the Lord,
That I even made it was a miracle!

My head was battered.
My body, mind, psyche & dreams
were shattered.
My losses lurked where I never felt before,
Penetrating deep down into my core.
I couldn't make sense out of my words,
Even simple things
seemed like nothing I'd ever heard.

I try not to think about it,
I don't want to get overwhelmed,
Then just quit.
I've got to keep going,
this is for sure,
I can't try to be
what I was once like before,

I reach out to friends and neighbors,
They help me get another look,
They aid me in realizing
the things I've mistook.

I do appreciate time with others,
But I cherish my time on my own.
Time to myself,
Time spent alone,
I need it,
It refreshes me,
I feed on it,
It blesses me.

It is when healing flow from within,
Time to allow broken wings to mend.

Lost in Thought

Confusion
Disarray
Commotion
Disorder

I breathe again

Oh yeah

What is my direction
On a wandering trail of feelings
Where did that time go
Off in space

My kitty rubs up against my leg

Oh yeah

Scramble

I was walking down the street one day,
My attention was far away,
Now I'm writing this message to you,
Yet part of me is in Kalamazoo -
I"m in a scramble,
My parts seem to ramble,
I'm trying to pull it all together
So I can take any sort of weather.
Aiming at my core,
My counselor helps me keep score,
We go over it
And over it again,
It'll sink into my skull,
I just don't know when.
Direction, goals and objectives,
I try to make it all corrective,
I'm developing persistence and constancy,
Seeing that I get all that I can from me.
I use my therapist as a resource,
She aids me in trying to keep on course,
I align myself
Paddle and catch the wave,
Lean into it,
Carve down the face,
I'm in the flow.
Nature aligns
Even those who are turned out,
Beauty, glory and grace win out!

Morlee Griswold, Ireland- World Kayak Surf Championship
Photo by Jono Stevens

Paved Paradise

I guess Joni Mitchell
was pretty right on,
When she said
that we'll never know
what we've got
until it's gone.
Does that mean
we don't usually appreciate our A, B or C
until they're taken from us?
I ask - does this have to be true?
Can you possibly imagine
that this has happened to you...?

In the flash of a moment,
the picture perfect sky
cracks into millions of tiny pixels.
The sun boils, blisters,
Pops and oozes dry.
The sedatory crash of the ocean waves
Turns to high-pitched wails.
Shock sets in,
Melody siphons into monotone,
Life's intimacies are dulled,
Processing slows,
Everything changes
In a blink of circumstance.
Pains cringe out of unknown places,
Emotions turn up their volume,
How you are now is not the same
as how you once were.
Now deal with it!

Smoke comes out of the tractor's exhaust...
Your paradise has been paved
and they're installing a parking lot.

In time,
You'll be looking for a parking space,
and you'll never know
what was once there in that place.
Worse yet and what's a scare,
You will not know what could have been there!

At first,
You probably don't realize
what you cannot do.
Just try to not let it get to you!

Brain injury flattens out our many capabilities,
Even ones that beforehand, we were not aware.
I guess some of us must learn these things the hard way -
The question remains...
Must we go through loss
To appreciate what was once there?
In you, I'm trying to cause a rustle,
So that you can exercise your empathy muscle!

To the unimpaired,
This is aimed,
So ignorance of this loss
will cease.
Knowledge births tolerance,
Acceptance...
For survivors deserve
To be granted their peace.

A clear portrait is being painted
of what we've got...
So don't belittle others,
Because what you can do,
they cannot.
Please...
Don't pave paradise and put up a parking lot!

(Joni Mitchell, 1970)

Sequelae

- Post-Traumatic Stress
- Memory
- Attending
- Mood Swing
- Psychosociality
- Melt Down
- Impulsivity
- Self-Importance
- Anger Management
- The O word
- Aphasia
- Light Sensitivity
- Anti-depressed
- Inhibition
- Moe

Sequelae

Brain injury is embroidered into a many-colored tapestry of consciousness. The background fabric is comprehensive; yet we are made up of our own stitching and colors. There is no arguing that we are all of one Spirit, but we are made of our own unique ingredients. Each of us is distinctly ourselves. The individualized molding of our personalities contours an injury to the brain. A brain injury is intimately shaped by our very makeup.

There is a vast array of possible sequelae (i.e. symptoms). There are some basic problems that almost all people with brain injury share (e.g. memory for example). An erratic array of pre-injury "issues" become exacerbated through a head trauma (and we all know that everyone has his/her own personal issues!) In this way, an injury is individualized. One survivor's injury is not replicated by another. There are many influences, some of them are: impact of injury (i.e. severity), location on the head and in the brain, age level at the time of incident and amount of time spent in a coma; these all affect the outcome of head trauma.

The resulting symptoms of injury to the brain are not at all understood or only superficially perceived by the general public. It was through my studies in Special Education for brain injury survivors[v], that I obtained knowledge about the many different aspects or sequelae of injury. In this chapter, I will share with you quite a few of the ramifications of brain injury. No doubt there will be some you who have experienced a few of these symptoms yourselves; having had a taste of what I am talking about is a dynamic means of understanding.

> I know, I know...
> Most everyone
> Comes upon some of these problems
> In his or her own season,
> But this is to let it be known -
> That brain injury survivors
> At least have a reason!

As opposed to growing old and some of these symptoms develop, a brain injury survivor is fine one day and all of a sudden finds him/herself dealing with major loss and a severe transition. S/he is now a different person, needs to get to know her/himself anew, and has to struggle with getting by in daily affairs.

In the movies, when a character has sustained a brain injury, things are *always* amiss! I want to speak some truth about what is involved in an injury to the brain. What are some of the resulting symptoms?

Post Traumatic Stress

Riding down the road,
Windows cracked open,
Music's playing,
Drifting off...
I catch myself,
Jam on the brakes!
- It's too late!

Immediate shock of adrenaline!
≈≈ Terror ≈≈
Out of control...

My world turns,
Rough tumbling,
Force,
Thrust,
Smack!
Through the windshield -
Stunned,
Shattered,
Flying...
Through space,
Into another world,
- Landing,
Lost in time,
Long suffering...

Post injury -
Years later,
Doing everyday errands,
Driving around town,
Memory flashes,
I get a feeling...
Embroidered deep,
Subconsciously instilled,
Out from the darkness it creeps.

Impressions awaken,
I get a taste of recall,
Subliminal messages become overwhelming,
Personal horror,
A shot out of the dark!

I lose myself in time,
Am I then or now?
It gets confusing, somehow.

Emotional scars,
Relived
Over and over again.

The insides go into replay,
Real life suspended in animation,
Only it's not funny!

Perspiration,
Wake up!
And the wheel turns...

Post Traumatic Stress

Memory

Brain injury may kindle some of your curiosity,
But you will never *fully* know
What it is to be
Without your memory.
"Know" in the Biblical sense,
Has to do with what you experience.

You can approach understanding
With the kindling empathy,
I will tell you what I experience,
To help you try to reach through
That awkward fence.

In my past…
Yesterdays,
Even todays,
Slipped by with only glimpses to grasp.
Recall names, incidents or locations of things,
Please - just don't ask.

Severity of loss
Will decrease all and all,
But at least a touch of this burden,
Is around for the long haul.

I've learned that memory is specific,
The array is vast.
Types of memory -
Need to be defined,
For between functions,
Is a distinct solid line:
Short term, Episodic, Autobiographical,
Long term, Prospective, Semantic and Procedural.
(For more info, see Glossary)

How is memory affected?
Some kinds may be devastated,
While others remain intact,
Recall can become cloudy,
Thinking unclear,
Sometimes I feel not fit -
But that's life,
I've just come to deal with it!

It's an issue for me,
To try and remember where things are.
Sometimes I close my eyes,
And just wish on the night's star.
I've given a new name
To the King of Kings -
"Ultimate Retriever of Lost Things"!

Regarding my loss,
I try & look at it positively,
And see it straight,
My stumbling with memory
Has led me to
A true stepping up of faith.

Attending

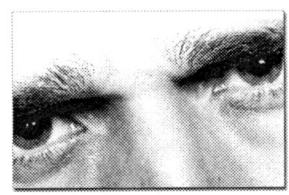

Deficit?
Not necessarily,
Preoccupied perhaps...
I'm selectively attending.

Input in overload,
There's a lot of information to choose from,
They consider it a deficit,
I consider it multiple attendances.
My many interests magnetize my attention,
- Perhaps I am a curious person.
Personal focus sways with the wind.

Does it disable me?
Or give me multiple abilities?
Diverse interests...
Various skills,
- No doubt,
But the question is,
Do I ever get anything done?

Punctually impaired,
Scattered...
It gets kind of personal.

I try to buckle down,
Get proactive,
Keep on track,
Concentrate, direct, dedicate,
I strengthen my will.

In action,
Doing ...
Today,
Not tomorrow,
It'll get done,

NO,
I'll get it done.

Mood Swing

Moonstone,
Clouded transparency of the heart,
A state of mind, emotion or feeling,
With a slippery territory
I seem to be dealing.
I'm relating to myself anew.
Erratic relations
Within myself,
As well as with others too,

Sparks of fire
Simmer in my icy brew.
No rules to obey -
I'm led to feel as I may,
I impulsively skid,
Love to anger,
Contentment to loneliness,
Then back to acting like a kid.

We may skip around,
Avoiding the issues for a while.
Although lurking...
In the shadows of the mind
Lay anger, depression,
Emotional aggression.
Rehabilitation -
We are our own guide.
Out of responsibility,
We must look inside.

What is curative for me,
- Is not putting stoppers on my feelings,
Finding a personal balance
Is what I find to be most healing.

Immersed
In rehab's self-rectification,
I distance the world,
Sink into isolation,
The busyness of the world
Gets kind of loud,
I tend to pull back,
Draw away from the crowd.

My sense of self at times gets confused,
Often belittled and self-abused,
My worst enemy gets a little loud...
To myself I think I am nothing,
No matter how well I am endowed.

And there I am...
Depression hovering,
Loneliness etched inside,
There's no need for pretend,
I sometimes wonder
When this ride is going to end.

I strive not to be crippled
by my own curse,
I wipe my tears and realize -
It could be much worse.

I turn on the radio,
And drown myself in music....

Psychosociality

It's really hard to understand
How a person is affected psychosocially,

The realms of distress are:
Emotional, social, behavioral and psychological.

These symptoms are less obvious to the average eye,
They are more enduring and harder to pacify,

The following is a seemingly endless inventory
Of survivors' ongoing obstacles:

- Increased emotionality
- Poor self-awareness
- Being socially inappropriate
- Frequent mood changes
- Being unmotivated or seeming to be of no use
- Reacting with alcohol and drugs
- Social disinhibition
- Depression
- Self-esteem disintegrates
- Loneliness
- Egocentricity/self-importance
- Anxiousness
- Impulsivity
- Decreased sense of discernment or judgment
- Poor anger management
- Insensitivity to others
- Unawareness of how actions impact others
- Lessened ability to interpret emotions & read situations
- Lowered tolerance for frustration

(List continues in Appendix C)

This is a somewhat complete list,
But no doubt,
There's some that I've missed.

Please take a little advice,
About what to give the survivor,
- How to supportively console:
Encourage strengths (e.g. sports, music or crafts),
So s/he won't over-identify with the "sick role".

Lastly,
After the continuous self-renovation of rehab,
**Please don't underestimate the power of your LOVE,
And positive feedback!**

Melt Down

Depression...
Deflates me,
Frustrates me,
Invalidates me,

I fluctuate,
Wander into self-hate,
Tend to isolate,
Myself,
I usually underrate,

I need someone to...
Medicate,
Vindicate,
Tolerate,

I am real,
and I feel,
But don't see the beauty
that is within me.
I am an infidel to myself.

I'm smoked,
I can't see through my fog,
I'm being charbroiled,
Churned,
Melted down.

It's like...
I tore my flesh out of my ribcage,
I'm scarred,
Hurting,
I wallow inside,
Watching my heart pulse and quiver -

Want to reach in,
Pull out my fear,
Only I clutch hold of the meds,
I confess,
I am a bit afraid
of where my depression has led.

It wraps into the subconscious
like a snake,
Even my strongholds
I let it take.
I avoid everything that makes me feel good,
Then there's no chance
of feeling like I could.

I'm simmering,

I walk my path alone.
I've yet to find someone
that harmonizes with my tone.
I want to tell you -
Self-esteem can be hard to inflate
all on your own.

I tell myself -
My attitude is my ammunition.
Good or bad,
It's my decision.

I swing from that moody tree,
But I'm losing grasp of the vine.
Personal importance stabilizes,
But mine is waning.
My strength of self is draining.

I'm liquefying,
Simmering, frying,
I ruminate about dying,

I'm melting down.

Impulsivity

I sometimes make decisions
in a bit of a hurry,
Initiated on a whim,
I tend to look back and worry.

I guess I react on my feelings,
Without giving myself
a chance to think
that it might not be so appealing.

I just think what I say...
Afterwards I wonder
Was that OK?

Down the road, I think –
"I would never have foreseen
that it might turn out this way!"

Perhaps I need to modify
how I react to things,
but it's tricky.
I don't want what I feel
to be buried in cement,
To find what's best for me
I need to experiment.

I simply live and learn.
From my mistakes
I come to better discern.

I'm told -
the more I structure my day,
The less time to be lured
to act in that rash sort of way.

Perhaps, at times
my actions do spring out of the blue -
That's exactly why I see a therapist -
To help me strategize
how to think it all through!

Self-Importance

Rehabilitation in process...
I withdraw into my shell,

For in order to be my own self-mechanic,
I have to attend to internal dynamics.

Well, where does that leave me?
→ Focused on **myself!**

Life revolves around me
And my injury,

I **AM** the center.

I know where my importance lays,
It's bottled up on my insides.

Some say I am simply absorbed in me,
Perhaps they think I have distorted priorities,

Emblazoned in my own world,
Relatively nothing out there seems of much importance.

It's not that I don't care
about things out there,

I just get overcome
by simply trying to get things done!

~~((*))~~
Impairment to the master organ,
I need to step up to the plate.
Certainly you would agree,
For it is I that needs to rehabilitate me!

But...
I don't want you to think it's all about self-possessing,
I can see how my injury has truly been a blessing!

Even amidst my inner turmoil,
Therapy has brought me a richer soil,

Rehab has taught me about self-repair,
It's taken a lot of work and a steady prayer!

And it certainly has given some interesting reading,
For all of you out there who are up for the feeding! ☺

Anger Management

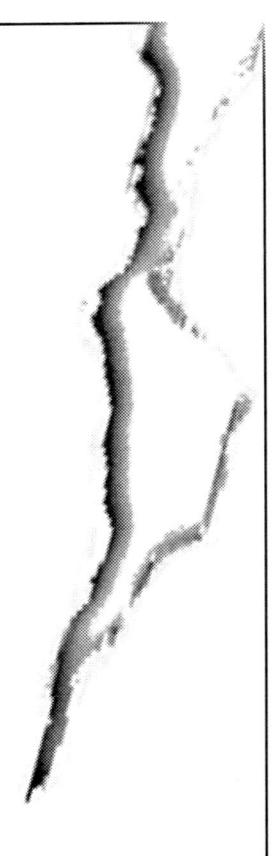

Tide rises,

Swells become more intensified,

Side-swiped by feelings,

Harsh winds gust off of my ocean,

Movement from harmony,

Seething furls of force,

OUT OF CONTROL!

Caught up in the rage,

Oh Lord, this too shall pass…

I try and take a moment for myself.

Breathe myself through the flames,

I unleash hold on my exhale,

Try and peep through the fumes,

There is a bigger picture…

Another deep breath,

…I can and will be open to love,

Mercy be with me,

And now,

I am in control.

The O Word

Disarranged,
Perpetually tied in knots,

Frontal lobe-kabob,
MY EXECUTIVE WAS FIRED,
(Executive skills - see Glossary)

My sense of order
seems to be across the border.

I'm seeking organization
that I can't grasp,

It's an unsightly disorder,
Takes so long just to complete a task.

I need to engage more of myself
just to keep me in line,

I call it the O word.
Like it's bad,
Don't say it,
I don't even want to think about it!

OrgAnize,
I realize,
I criticize,
Scrutinize,
Self-antagonize,
Can't fit in that orderly size,
I must compromise,

Or else...
I'll try to strategize:
Categorize,
Visualize,
Compartmentalize,
Itemize,
Familiarize,

Otherwise –
I'll just improvise.

OrgAniZe

Aphasia

Expressive Aphasia

It's on the tip of my tongue,
I know exactly the meaning
of what I'm looking for...
Uuhhh!!!
Mental strain
Constipation of the mind,
...And nothing comes,
I know that if I turn off my inner talk,
It is more likely to emerge
from the depths of my subconscious.

Me,
Personally,
I've come to see,
I reap the benefits
of this strain to my mental muscle.
I put it in high gear,
In the mode of must find,
I strive for articulation of my mind.

This is where my poetic yearning did begin,
Wild striving into memory,
Mentally and emotionally,
I'd scan universes beyond my origin,
Reach in and pin down my feelings,
Capture that thought
and write it down.

Yes, I said I'd write it down,
Just as was encouraged in rehab,
For memory's sake!
Strengths manifest
out of the fires of rehabilitation.
Expression on command,
My semantic dream,

... **Aphasic return**

Receptive Aphasia

What you talkin' about, girl?
(Aphasia- see Glossary)

Light Sensitivity

I close my eyes
yet it is still bright

I can't seem to hide myself
from the light

of course
I need the light
to focus in
otherwise
I prefer my home
to be lit rather dim

others may think
my mode is
kind of glim
but if I run my life
by how others want it
I will never win

perhaps I have an inner glow
I see it as an asset
not an obstacle

I like to say
I darken the outer lights
so you can see my inner sparkle

Anti-Depressed

I've surrendered to the fact,
My depression isn't always
white or black.
With this dark cloud
I seem to be hexed,
Ranging from mild
to almost obsessed.

I'm tired of
the ups and downs,
My counselor
made me come around,
She said -
If it was simply a physical ill,
I probably wouldn't hesitate
in taking the pills.

I just don't want to feel
like on the meds
I've got to stay,
From them,
I'm always trying to get away.
Dependency sucks,
Yet this seems to be my ill luck,
For now, anyway,
There seems to be no other way.

Head injury does have this twinge,
Anti-depressants help me not to cringe,
For months I've been constantly taking my share,
Now it's not taking me all the way there.

Footprints in the sand grow deeper,
Medical restraints need grow steeper,
I explained to my psychiatrist
the meds were starting to not come close,
He understood and increased my dose.

Now I feel strong the suppression
of my persistent depression.
It's not at all a natural feeling
with which I am presently dealing.
I'm so used to the waves of my own turf,
Now it's flat waters and *there is no surf!*

Depression has been dissolved,
Biologically sedated,
Flat,
Monotone,
Dead as a stone.

This is hard for me to explain,
Without you thinking I'm insane,
You see -
I don't feel the ups and downs anymore,
But I still feel the inner ramblings
I would experience before.

I go through actions,
I know my dismal reactions,
I have remnants
of depressed responses in my head,
My internal conversations
In the subconscious
they were imbed.

I still feel my knee jerking,
Even without the depression lurking.
I recall the emotional waves
in which I was engrossed;
I hear those mental meanderings,
Just like a ghost!

It's haunting, jaunting,
Dis-settling, unnerving,
Now I realize
how all of this would enslave,
For out of these depressed ramblings,
I would incessantly behave.

Oh Lord, I wish I could have a subconscious sedation,
Perhaps I just need to change my medication!

Inhibition

The other day
I got a fortune cookie;
Wisdom in a tasty package...
"Love all, trust a few."

Well, I've learned hard,
Repeatedly,
If I must say,
From giving trust where it isn't due...
Inhibition can be my friend.

I want to trust,
→ Love,
But I want to protect myself!
LOVE SAVES and...
Inhibition can be my friend.

Trust -
I wrap it in a package,
So I can learn to put personal value to it.
In fettering my trusting of others -
My regard for myself fills up.
Self-esteem slowly completes itself.
Inhibition can be my friend.

I can't just blindly give it away,
I don't want my heart
to be in a free falling,
uncontrollable,
sliding board ride.
I want to be in control,
Taking action,
Not be in reaction,
Inhibition can be my friend.

I've put my trust up on a sacred shelf.
To be pulled down,
It needs to be earned!
In my walk,
I have learned
to trust in the Lord,
But should I trust people?
...Inhibition can be my friend.

The clouds float by,
It's all good.

Moe

Out of the corner of my eye,
I see that masked man,
Darting around corners,
Slinky red cape flying,
He seems magnetized
To where he needs to be...
Funny,
I find him pretty often
To be around me!
I'm sure it's obvious to him
That I am squandering,
Endlessly meandering.
I try to be alert to his hidden presence.
I must beware...
He's going to plug me in!
Who does he think he is?
Tony Robbins?
He conceals his persona,
Hides behind circumstances,
Makes me think it's all me,
He sets off my inner trigger,
With that mischievous twinkle in his eye,
Tolerant smile.

Moe

Go!
Let it flow,
When I trash my excuses,
He helps me reach a new plateau.
He knows...
How brain injury causes us to not want to go.
He often goes on tiptoe.
I can't always tell
When he's knocking on my do'.
He gets me going,
For this.
Him I owe.
I'll ride a rodio
If I think I can do so.

Moe T.

He wants a little more from me,
I have come to agree.
Success -
He wants me to climb that tree,
Even when I need adaptability.
He helps me not see deficiency.
For is the cup half filled
Or half empty?
It all depends
On how I choose to see.
He encourages me not to hold back,
Even when others think that skills I lack.

In me,
He causes a stir,
Through lessons inferred.
He presses on my accelerator.
Gets me to feel
That it's a touch of nature,
Drives me to be
MASTER ARTICULATOR,
He knows a way to push each of us
To be greater.
Wants it now,
Not later,
He is...

Moe T. Vator ! [vi]

Rehabilitation

- Celebration
- Metacognitive
- The Unpaved Road
- Survivor
- Invisible Disability
- Peer Counselor
- Visioning
- Inner Cave
- Riding on G-d's Plan
- Closure
- Healing
- "Disabled"
- Rehabilitative Exercise
- Life Moves
- Keeping the Faith

Rehabilitation

This is a virtual picture of me taken in the hospital, during the acute phase of my rehabilitation. In the picture, it shows virtually how I felt - semi-warped. I went through two rehab hospitals and then was transferred to an outpatient rehab. At the outpatient rehab they helped me become more able to communicate and perform functional life skills. Rehabilitative services are crucial in the acute and post-acute stages of injury (Acute Rehabilitation – see Glossary). If not received at that time, it becomes a whole lot harder down the road.

We must question, what is rehabilitation? For a brain injury survivor, it becomes a lifestyle, an increased awareness; rehabilitation involves the act of redeveloping an introspective awareness of one's new self and behavior. What is needed is a willingness to adapt (i.e. that means willfully changing yourself). in the interaction with others. Adaptive intelligence is a necessary personal ingredient for someone surviving a head trauma. Therapists can better work with survivors if they realize that change is part of the equation and don't too fervently resist it.

The development of brain injury survivors involves life skills, psychosocial, cognitive as well as neurological rehabilitation. Many difficulties lay in the simple, functional, every day world. Life skills rehab helps a person to be more functionally independent. "Psychosocial" refers to the social, emotional, behavioral and psychological dynamics of brain injury (this is quite a lot in a nutshell). Working with a peer counselor/special educator or rehab counselor is what I find to be most affective in dealing with issues in each of these categories. My personal experience has been that when I was counseled by a person who had a brain injury herself, I found the results to be more profoundly affective. When a therapist has experiential understanding regarding what the client may be going through, s/he can then best help the client to strategize about ways to approach the situation because of his/her own personal understanding.

Cognitive rehabilitation can be approached in various ways depending on the results sought after. This can be from formal cognitive retraining (e.g. on the computer or programs such as PACE - Processing and Cognitive Enhancement), working with executive skills with someone trained in the field, or just spending time with family or friends with thought processes that a survivor finds challenging. Other means of treatment can be medication, support groups as well as love and support from friends and family; all of these can play a critical role in rehabilitation.

We will now touch upon a neurological aspect of traumatic brain injury rehabilitation which the public is less familiar with; this is regarding the dysfunction of the Tempero-Mandibular Joint (TMJ) and the flattening out of the cervical curvature of the spine. These impairments result from the jolting of the head and spine at the time of impact. A very large amount of nerves going back and forth between the body and brain go through the jaw; both the trigeminal neural complex, located adjacent to the TMJ, and the jaw are compromised. Nervous rebounding initiated by this dysfunction, occur throughout the body causing compensatory pains, imbalances in posture and gait (See Appendix D).

Finally, it is important to note that there are positive psychological developments that take place in rehabilitation (for more information, see Greatest Advantage of Having a Head Injury in the last chapter). In my perspective, the following are some ways in which survivors are edified:

- Many survivors eventually become more in touch with themselves and others.
- After accepting personal limitations, a person tends to develop a more accepting attitude.
- A person may have to let go of the need to control, because that individual will probably find him or herself severely lacking the ability to control his or her behavior.
- When some functions are absolutely devastated, it is common for survivors to find new, previously unrecognized strengths.
- A person develops a certain "realness". The tendency is for brain injury survivors to enter more into the immediacy of the moment or present centered living and tend to draw more from their heart.

Celebration

It's Mom's birthday,
A day to rejoice in her arrival,
It's a day for living to celebrate,
Also a day to give praise for my survival,

It's been fifteen years,
It seems there's no more gloom to clear,
No, not this year,
No urgency,
No tears,
Less need to reflect,
No hidden pains to dissect,

I'm building a new life,
Less dependency,
Less strife.
It gets cold
And alone,
In pulling away,
From habits I've known.

The day's meaning I actually forgot,
Mom called and reminded me,
How she's grateful,
That me she's got,
And that I'm here,
To celebrate another year...

The toils & strife that I've endured,
I've earned the right to be heard..
I smile knowingly and sweetly,
Feeling ready to approach new frontiers,
Because I've survived
Fifteen years.

Metacognitive

Introspective complications,
Self-awareness is compromised,
I must get to know myself anew,
What are my limitations?
What are my needs?
What are my strengths?
- New landscapes to explore.

How do I get it done?
What will help me?
Cues?
Repetition?
Notes to myself?
Adaptive devices?

~~((*))~~

I must problem solve,
Accommodate,
Strategize,
DO I PERCEIVE WHAT IS EFFECTIVE?

Support groups
Supply mirrors to myself.
Self-evaluation,
Emerging awareness of deficits,
Are attitudes getting in my way?
AM I AWARE OF HOW I AM AWARE?[iv]

Introspective thinking,
I begin to see light at the end of the tunnel.
I start to understand
how my deficits
prevent me
from achieving my goals.

**THE FIRST STEP IN ALLEVIATING A PROBLEM,
IS COMING TO REALIZE THERE IS A PROBLEM.**

The Unpaved Road

It's been quite some time
I've been traveling on this route,
No one ever told me
What it was all about,
I've been probed to my core,
Sometimes I wonder
What it's all for,

I'm affected on the inside
Morning, noon and night,
My friends and family
Say it will be all right.
But what do they know?
They've never been down this road,
All they know
Are the impressions that I've showed.

Oh Lord,
Help me.
No one ever told me
How complex all of these difficulties would be.
There are no signs pointing the way,
How can people say it'll be Ok?

They may know of my problems with memory,
But they couldn't possibly know
How widespread it affects me!
What about my sense of disorientation
And the disappearance of my dreams?
How come no one ever told me about these things?

There are potholes along the road,
My abilities have seemed to corrode,
No one ever paved this road for me,
I trip over obstacles I can't even see,
Sometimes,
I feel the doctors are only guessing,
I think
Some may need
More knowledge and skill
To be assessing!

I don't want the doctor
To paint the picture
What my outcome will be…
He may be having a bad day,
I believe much more in me!

I may be making it up as I go,
But I best accommodate for myself,
This I know.
I trust in my instincts,
Get a little help along the way,

Trauma to the brain,
Neurological traffic,
...Blocks do let up
Along the unpaved road.

Symptoms abounding:
Behavioral,
Emotional,
Sense of self,
Psychosocial,
Cognitive,

Untying knots,
Braiding myself back together,
Rehabilitation.

Therapy -
Knowledge rebounds in the aftermath,
Recognizing new parts of myself,
Healing is in flow,
Internalizing,
Developing,
I'm traveling down that road.

Survivor

We're on the move,
Despite obstacles.
In active pursuit,
Holding firmly onto a purpose,
Individualized triumphs,
Emotional travail,
It gets kind of personal.
Survivor

Needing to compensate
Leads us
To examining ourselves,
Continuously,
In depth,
The inner eye of rehab,
Always watching,
24-7,
Stay awake
Or more therapy it'll take.

Not a victim of tragedy,
Over-comer of functional challenges,
Every day - getting by in the world,
Struggling toward independence,
Even amidst the walls of crumbling self-worth,
Inner torment...
Survivor

Our cards have been dealt,
We're working with our hands,
Challenges,
Inner battles,
Finding a balance,
Building character,
Standing strong,
We try to not
Let our weaknesses
Harm our self-concept.
Rehab is the fitness trainer of the self.
Repetitive sets of self-alteration,
Improvement (?)
Do beware -
A critical mind
Never fully loves itself.

Don't swallow it
Hook, line and sinker!
Mustn't we consider
Forgiving ourselves
Our wrongs?

As we accept each other as is,
Drops of love trickle down,
Leaving us richer in depth,
Helping us to heal,
A touch of faith...

Survivor

Invisible Disability

I acutely dreamed
what it would be like to be
without remnants
of a disability.

Inwardly struggling,
yet outwardly not showing it,
can be a deception
to the world...

Others look and see -
they don't know
what things are like for me,
...don't know what it's like
to walk in my shoes,

SILENTLY...
THE EPIDEMIC ENSUES.

It's good and it's bad,
I don't want everyone
knowing my business,
and they don't know -
from what I show,
unless I choose
to tell them though.

...I guess I've reached my dream,
but it's not always as glorious
as it may seem!

I'm always struggling with me,
depression, anger management, memory...
sometimes my insides
are a bit up-stirred,
this often leaves me
feeling not so self-assured.
I'm really not complaining
about my life's lot,
personal assets aren't measured
by what I have not!
with some things missing...
I sure do appreciate
what I've got!

To myself,
I assuredly insist,
I am the executive of my life,
discerning for myself,
decision maker,
planner,

Frontal lobe goulash,
injured -
but making my way,
Corrective,
Not self-accusative.
I am only
what I claim myself to be.

Invisible disability

Peer Counselor

I just want to fill you in,
On what others could not even begin,

She is so there for me,
Perhaps I just need someone to listen patiently,

She "knows" brain injury,
I think she can understand me,

She's my peer,
She's one that's got it in gear,

She can see what's going on inside,
She supports me on my ride,

Advocate,
We share a laugh,

Intercessor,
She pleads on my behalf,

Her care flows to me,
So naturally,

Fully cognizant of trauma to the head,
She's helped me to weave my own little web,

We've worked together through some hard times
Just like a team,

She's even pointed me
Toward going after some of my dreams!

As a peer and counselor,
She helps me with my self-esteem,

With goals, objectives & a little love,
She intervenes,

Her peer support has come to mean so much,
And so many people her job does touch! [vii]

Visioning

Once upon a time...
Everything was going my way,
My personal plans were interrupted,
What more can I say?

I guess it's not always
what you can see,
Years I had to put into
rebuilding me,

I've been walking this path
without a distinct plan,
I sometimes wonder
if I'm being all that I can,

I believe
we are what we make ourselves to be,
Otherwise,
I could blame anyone but me.

I could have tried
to do what is expected of me,
But perhaps, others
I will never fully please,

My strengths and abilities
have significantly changed,
My goals
I now need to rearrange.

Rehab has worked
at cultivating my soil,
I will now plant my ambitions
and make them uncoil.

I've got to get straight
about building my dream -
For it's only as important
as I make it seem.

Accomplishing a dream
is not like getting a dessert,
It means focusing your efforts
and doing the work.

When talking about this subject,
it does get grammatical,
In picturing "dreaming",
- People think of floating off in Na-Na Land
and taking a sabbatical.

"Visioning" is more proactive,
- more realistic,
In planning my life,
It allows for the artistic.

I fortify what I envision
with the fuel of attention,
Keeps me away
from my apprehensions,

Going after my dreams is a reality,
Not an abstract hope;
It takes tiny steps,
Just like climbing a rope.

The first move,
In order to bring it into form,
To try and make it whole,
Is to turn my dreams
into set out goals.

From there,
I break it down
on my own elective,
Into little baby doable objectives.

That way,
I am accomplishing something
it seems,
Not just abstractly
"Going after my dreams".

I'm trying to turn myself
to positive self-talk,
So I will follow through
and make this plan walk.

~~~((*))~~~
At one time,
Life may have deflated me,
Left me dry,

Now,
I'm pumping up my vision,
So I can fly!

Inner Cave

Withdrawn,
Into myself,
Walls are projected,
Boundaries,
I'm on guard,
Taking care of myself.

My cave draws me in
(and keeps you out),
You would think
It would be a place of rest...

Oh, it is a place of unrest.
All that I shut out
Torments me inside.
I close my eyes,
Believe that peace is possible.

Pains hide themselves from me,
There is agony inside my stuffy cave,
- Some openings in the rock
Let the light peep in.

There is a door
Carved into the wall,
If I were to unlock it,
- Peril lurks,
Perhaps I have to take a risk...
I want to unbolt myself,
Need to let my demons out,

Need to reconcile with myself,
I have natural boundaries inside,
I trust in the Lord's protection,
No one can steal that from me.

The air inside my cave is stale.
I crack open the door,
Unlock myself,
Fresh air caresses my skin,
My shoulders uncringe,
I take a deep breath,
I leave my door swaying in the breeze,

And the wind blows through.

Riding on G-d's Plan

Vroom, Vroom...
Revving up,
The engine has a sacred hum,

Carrying us in any direction -
Up, down, north, south, east or west,
I just know
That all the questions inside,
Will be answered on the ride.

It's not always a smooth ride for any of us,
Tested in trauma,
Weathered with persistence,
We've got to stay strong,
Got to carry on,

My sister once said to me
"Girl, you're floating on the wings of Jabez,
Blessed, oh blessed,
You've been indeed,
Accepting and loving yourself,
Together with the Holy Ghost,
He's graciously expanded your territory,
Enlarged your coast.

His hand is with you and it is good,
Protecting you from evil,
As a loving Father would." [viii]

I know that He knows
My insides,
Even better than I do.
Yet He loves me as I am,
To change...
I don't even need to.

G-d's sacred plane comes in and prepares to land,
All is according to His Master plan.
(See Appendix A)

Closure

Healing of old wounds,
Bandages on the heart.

Wrapped around,
Sealed tight,

Unscrew the cap of the mind,
Just loosen where it won't unwind,

Salve of the Self,
Reach in and apply,

Inner fulfillment,
The LOVE is given to take us there.

Consciously accepting,
Appreciating just as is,

Psychological scars,
Imprints erased,

Not looking,
But saved,

The rhythm slows,
The circle is made whole.

Objective perspective -
Looking through the window at myself,

Peeling out from inside of me,
Regenerating my core,

The chapter ends,
Complete within itself,

Transitioning to the next...
Potent possibility.

Healing

Loss,
Leads to...

Picking ourselves up,
Putting the pieces back together,

The brain tries to fix things that don't work,
Healing happens on it's own accord,

Spontaneous recovery,
Nature's handy work,

I'm recreating me,
Designing my lifestyle anew,

And I'm doing it...
Functional mathematics,

With a style of my own,
I'm actively completing the puzzle,

I always win
By keeping a positive attitude,
And a SMILE! ☺

Perhaps with only a tinge of motivation,
I reload myself,

Boot myself up,
Connect to the Cosmic Computer.

I find my own way that gets me by,
Unique to just I,

Creatively, I compensate,
So I just don't leave my disability to the act of fate.

Contouring accommodations,
To my idiosyncrasies,

I cracked the mold,
Now, I'm reinventing myself.

Flexibility of spirit,
Allowing me to be as need be,

The cards may have been dealt,
But nothing is set in stone,

I'm fighting the fates,
In for another round,

And now
I'm creating my own!

I will not let myself
Be hampered by my injury,

Oh no,
It does not define me!

I will not allow myself
To succumb to "come what may",

When things go wrong,
I just do it a different way,

I try to always remember,
The Healer is on call,

He just needs to be asked
To help us stand tall.

"Disabled"

I must analyze
The definition of this word,
For the underlying meaning
Is somewhat absurd.

Disabled?
Do you mean UN-abled?
No, not me,
To that I say "hey!"
I'll get through that obstacle,
My own little way.

Are you diss-ing me,
Just because I have trouble
With my memory?

Please understand,
I don't think that I'm so great,
I've just learned to compensate.

We're moving on in time,
For sure,
"Handicapped" isn't politically correct
Anymore.

People with a disability
Are not handicapped,
Not necessarily passive,
Potential is there to be tapped.

Our challenges
We want you to understand,
But in your mind,
Don't put us in the "handicap" brand.

We're in a different time,
It's a different paradigm,

We look at ourselves
In quite a different light,
We believe we can do
Almost anything we put in sight!

"Disabled"
If you assume my inability
Through this name...
ADA, IDEA,
My rights and integrity I can legally claim.

Overcoming challenges
Makes a person strong -
Strength in mind,
Togetherness in heart,
Help us to keep on keeping on!

Rehabilitative Exercise

A catalyst for reformation,

Trauma is digitally stored
In our complex holistic machinery,
A state of disequilibrium ensues,
Vulnerability seeks a plug,
Need to seek a balance.

Brain injury →
Mind's connection with the body
Off kilter,
Loses tight grip,
Proprioception,
Visual impairments,
Loss of balance,
Postural abnormalities,

We must pull from the depths,
Train the core of the soul -
Awareness,
Adaptability,
Patience,
Persistence,
Endurance,
Equilibrium.
Physical exercise -
Reawaken dormant brain cells,
Stimulate the functioning of the mind,[ix]

Bridge the disconnect,
Conscientious balancing,
Corrective postural cues,
Strengthen
Lengthen
Gentle Pilates.

Sedimentation of unused bodily tissue,
WAKE UP!
Refresh the "core",
Invigorate and release holds,
Free up the joints,
Facilitate movement,
Elongate the spine,
Persistence,
Practice,

Holistic integration,
Develop a "core" understanding of alignment,
Come to perceive with rehabilitative eyes,
Learning is not all in your head (Hannaford, Carla 1995).

Check the research -
Movement is critical
For the relief of depression.
Clears obstructions,
Lifts the mood.

Pilates –
In the Flow,
Feng Shui of the body, mind and heart,

Withdraw dependency on the therapist,
Take little baby steps of responsibility,
Self-implemented therapy.

Where there's a will,
There's a way!

Life Moves

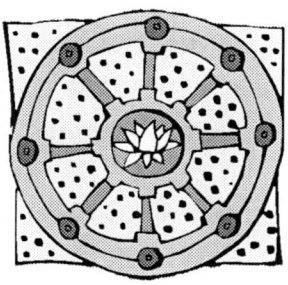

The wheel spins...
In each direction,
North, South, East & West,
Up, down, out & in,

The planets go on their celestial course,
Seasons fuse one into another,
The earth goes around the sun,
A new day dawns,
Existence is in flow,
Time goes on.

Rivers and oceans,
Eddy and flow,
Provide the rhythms of life
as we know,
Tide comes in,
Tide goes out,
Swells scratch the bottom,
Rise into waves,
Nature makes room
for us to play.

Flowing on course,
We are all interconnected,
Lovers magnetize each other,
They say two hearts
are better than one,
Love blossoms,

Husband & wife,
Come together,
Sprout a new life,
Children blossom,
Freshen our world,

After life springs anew,
We get caught up in the wonder
of whatever our children do.
Kids - they wake us up deep inside,
Bring us back to really living,
They make even Granny and Grandpa
feel young and swinging!

There is a depth of beauty
even amidst the process of aging,
Perhaps the American dream
needs a little changing!

No doubt,
There's the wrinkles and crankiness
that comes in time's race,
But let's not deny
Dignity, wisdom & grace.

The eye of the beholder
Needs a contact lens
To better see -
Inner strength
Builds on facing challenges.
Time buys distinction and honor.

Health circulates,
Capillaries, Arteries, Veins,
Cycle of nourishment,
Distributing vitality to the cells,
Into the heart,
Returning to the cells once more,

Cerebrospinal fluid flows,
from the head to the spine,
and back again.
On its own rhythm,
Millions of nerves find their way,
All accommodating as they may.

Left on their own,
Injuries mend themselves.
"Time heals all wounds"
is what they say,
To a certain degree, anyway.

Healing happens.
There's nothing cliché about it,
Though we may not return
to how we were before,

Please consider
"different" can work better,
Fresh treasures are found
going down new corridors.

Support groups -
Regally supply
the attention one needs,
The kind that even friendships
don't necessarily feed,
For it is when we come together,
We can enable one another.

All aspects of life
Moving,
Changing,
Developing and evolving,
Children,
Senior citizens,
The injured,

The withering,
Waning,
And wise,
The struggling and stumbling,
Can be seen as beautiful,
in their own disguise.

We can focus in
and glimpse integrity
where it is not sought.
Touch upon a sweet virtue...
From which we all can be taught,

The omnipotent G-d
is just, merciful & wise,
The natural side of G-d
sees things with Her own eyes!
The whole solar system
Turns by their guide...

The Lord moves and develops
through each of us,
Churning and turning,
Expressing and blessing,
Healing is on call...
and is available to all,

Grab ahold.

Keeping the Faith

The battle-ax of head trauma -
Insidious depression.

It comes in waves,
I go into myself and try to ride it out,

Sometimes I just watch the tube,
To tune it all out.

I like days
With sweet, mellow waves.

Some swells are more forceful than others,
After a storm, clouds clear, depression wanes,
(S.A.D.-see Glossary)

Tides, winds, hormones, self-concept,
There is many an influence.

Warrioress of the sea,
I'm learning to ride all turbulence,

I can swim oceans of loneliness,
But it gets rough in the sea all alone,

Feeling lonesome can drip deep,
To the inner crevices it creeps,

I admit I have wandered into dreams of suicide,
But there I won't let myself reside.

What scares my mom is that I'd -
Be at home alone in that dark cavern inside.

But it is out on the water,
I know a peace that is all my own,

A natural comfort,
Almost as if I'm finding my way home.

I know that G-d's grace He does provide,
I'm trying to wake it up inside,

I'm looking to catch a better ride,
Maintaining an integrity that I can't hide,

I try to cope and understand myself,
Sometimes by the sea I am tossed,

Nevertheless,
I've got to keep the faith,
No matter what the cost!

~~((*))~~

Off the straight and narrow,
I try not to slide,

Because I've touched on somewhere better...
On the other side.

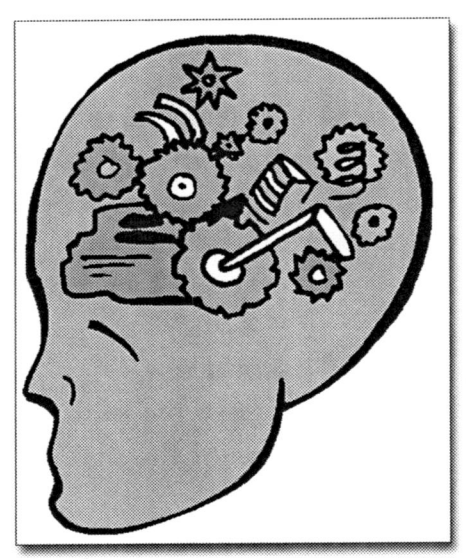

The Brain

- Master Organ
- Neuron
- Frontal Lobe
- Limbic System
- Left Hemisphere
- Right Hemisphere
- The Balance of the Poet

The Brain

An intricate, multi-faceted, many functioned organ facilitates our survival and development; without getting lost in technical jargon, I will discuss the complex and powerful master organ – the brain. Injury to the brain is a fascinating field of study, in it the field of science is becoming more conscious of the brain and it's functions. Through brain injury rehab, holistic intelligence is utilize - cognitive, psychological, social, emotional and intuitive intelligence; brain injury survivors need to touch on fuller use of their human capabilities.

Someone with a brain injury learns that we cannot dissect the holistic experience. The cerebral functions are interwoven neurologically with all parts of the body. My personal experience with the rebound affect of injury made me profoundly realize the intimate way the body and brain interact. Post-injury, I developed major colon and bladder problems; who would have ever thought that these organs would be so directly related to the functioning of the brain? When scientists categorize the brain into pieces, it is so we can simply try to understand our vast array of processes and how our brain functions. We must realize that we can only segregate these functions in our mind, as they are experientially inseparable.

The brain is closely allied with our spirit (e.g. the Central Nervous System can make us innately hyperactive or calm and centered). How we acknowledge and tend to our imbalances allows us to begin to gain control of how we conduct ourselves. Our will power is intricately interlaced with the functioning of the brain. What we do, how we think and behave, what we desire, how forcefully we desire it, how or if we go after goals, how we choose to appear, even our faith, all involve will power. The brain conducts who we are.

Master Organ

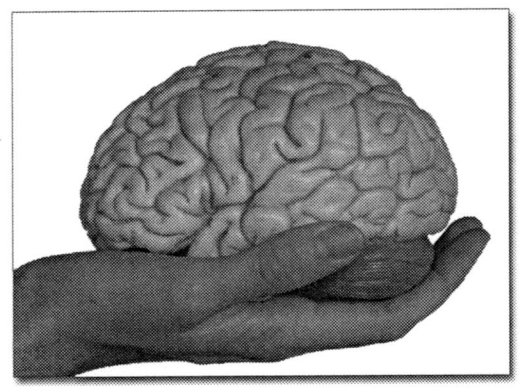

Infinite mind,
Intelligible cortex,
Neural networking,
All parts of the brain
Meshed into the whole,
Interconnected,
Complex,
Yet simple system,

Encased in a bony skull,
Protected and covered
by three membranes,
Outside ➔ in
The wrapping of a heavy plastic sheet,
Cob-webbing amidst the wrinkles and folds,
Tender molding in the crevices,
...Cushioned
Gelatinous mind.

Internal landscape,
Delicate nerve tissue,
Nurtured by vessels,
Flowing from the heart,
Circulating into the subconscious.

A good portion is hollowed out.
Fluid circulates,
Reservoirs of plenty,

Cerebro-spinal current,
Pulsing at it's own rhythm,
Flowing down the vertebral falls,

Cerebral
Wrinkles & crevices,
Distinguished into hemispheres,
In a dichotomized world,
Corpus Callosum
Bridges the differences.

The right side of the machine -
Neurologically connects
to the left side of the body.
- Left to right,
Impulses neurotransmit,
Leaping the gaps,

Lobes fenced off,
Accomplishing distinct functions,
Frontal, Temporal, Parietal, Occipital,
(for more info, see Appendix E),
Working together to get it all done.

In today's rush,
Cerebellum triggers movement,
Stem rooted into the chord of the spine.
Bundles of nerves,
Connecting,
Wiring together all our different parts,
Conducting the symphony of ourselves,

Intellectual, Emotional, Functional,
Physical, Psychological, Social,

Sensory, Intuitive,
Holistic, Multimodal,

Survival,
Evolution,

It's all in our head.

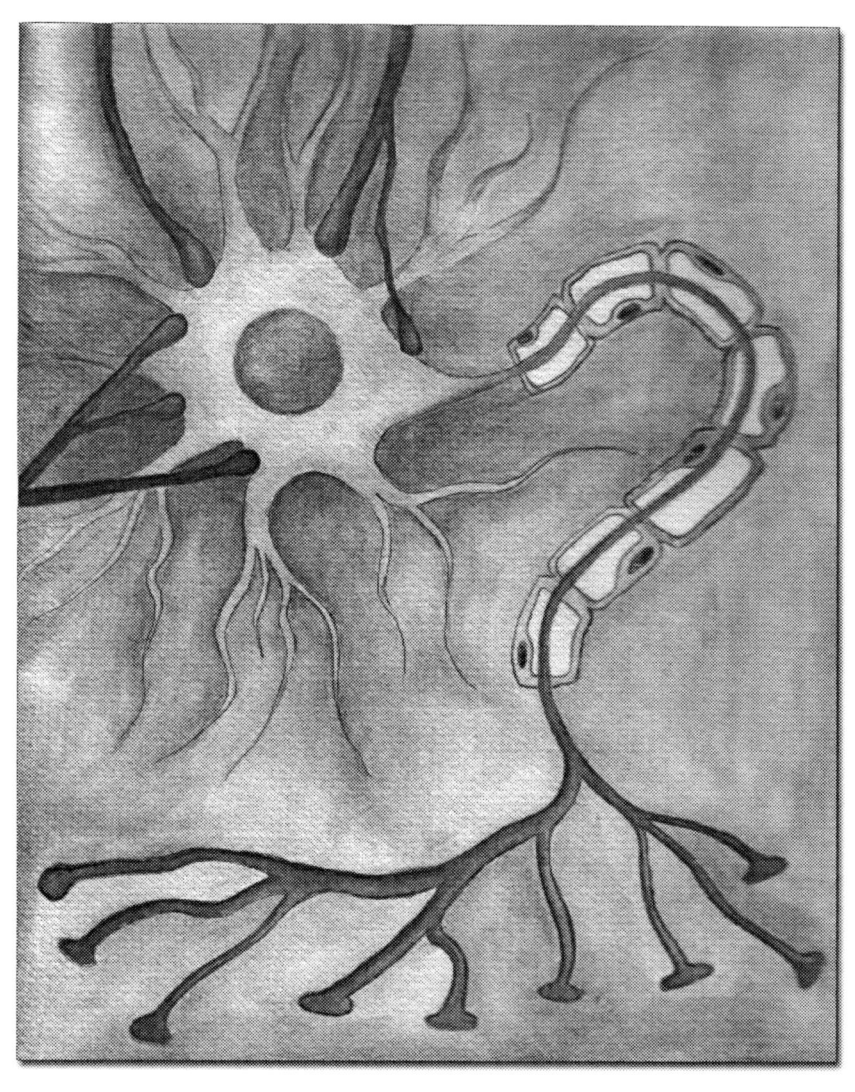

Heidi Lerner

Mind of the Machine

Neuron

Miniature information center,
Communicator,
Receives thousands of signals,
Every moment,
Decides to fire or not,
Blocks or surges,
Launches electrical impulses,
Dendrites – Short wavy neurological receptors,
Cell body – Neuronal intelligence,
Axon – Long slim wire,
Conducts signal from one cell to the next,
Synapse,
Junction,
Junction jumper,
Neurotransmitters interconnect,
Activated by what we eat,
Fueled by amino acids,
Synaptic health,
Whitewater rush of neurochemicals,
Eddy on this side,
Ferry across,
GO!
Body and mind,
In active communication,
Triggering or delaying,
All aspects of character,
Whole persona,
Body, mind and soul,
Acting as one,

Transmission of life,
Tiny cells,
Billions and billions,
Nervous system,

We're wired up.

Frontal Lobe

Impact,
Coup -
Cortex sloshes forward,
Up against the wall of the skull,
Contra coup -
Swishes back,
Jello shake,
Slushes into the skull's rough, bony surface.
Ripping, Tearing,
Scarring, Swelling,
Uh Oh!!!
Executive ruin,
(Executive skills – see Glossary)
And the walls come tumbling down,
Amidst the rumble:
Decision making,
Planning,
Organizing,
Assigning priorities,
Making decisions,
Initiating actions,
Behaving,
Interacting socially,
Inhibition,
Personality changes,
A person isn't like they once were.

Frontal lobe injury.

(See Appendix E)

Limbic System

Mammalian brain,
It's instinctual,
Emotions,
Basic drives,
Fear,
Hunger,
Sex,
Thirst,
Survival.

Hippocampus:
Crippled,
Hippo needs to go to the campus vet!
Like a pole to hang clothes on -
It stands no more.
Nowhere to store information,
Everything winds up all over the floor.
It's difficult to find memories you're looking for -
(Savage & Wolcott, 1994, p.21)
Information is hard to retrieve,

Amygdala:
Emotional memories,
Reading facial expressions and body language,
Reactions based on emotions,
Fight or flight!

Limbic injury
Disrupts how you perceive the world,
How you feel,

It gets complex.

Left Hemisphere

Linear,
Structured,
Analytic,
Observes details,
Alert watchfulness,
Attends to the pieces,
Notices differences,
Semantic,
Reading,
Writing,
Verbalizing,
Letters,
Sentences,
Grammatical intelligence,
Numbers,
Calculation,
Sequential thinking,
Procedures,
How to... A B C,
Planning,
Directing toward goals,
Future oriented,
Reaching an end,
Propositional thinking,
Technique,
Sports: Hand / eye / foot placement,
Art: Media / tool use / how to,
Music: Composing – notes / beat / tempo,
Controls feelings,

Left hemisphere.[x]

Right Hemisphere

Gestalt,
Nonlinguistic,
Perception of form,
Sees the whole picture,
Spatial orientation,
Emotion,
Meaning,
Intuition,
Flow,
Imagination,
Spontaneity,
Now-oriented,
Free thinking,
Sees similarities,
Estimates,
Simultaneous thinking,
Sports: Rhythm, flow,
Art: Abstract, imaging, emotion,
Music: Passion, rhythm, tone,
Fluidity,
Experiences feelings,

Right hemisphere [x]

(See Appendix E)

The Balance of the Poet

Semantic adventurer,
Warrioress of thought,
Pulling from the parts,
Yet envisioning the whole.
Stanzas of planned format
Leap out of the page at you
In spontaneous meaning.
With a plan to be spontaneous,
Linguistic artist,
Imprints her mind on the page,
Imagine that...
Her brush of thought
Paints feelings,
Her words show color,
Shaded by grammatics,
She paints an abstract mural,
Readers drink it in,
Enjoy and comprehend,
Simultaneous designs
Approach their minds.
Subconscious infiltration -
She plays educational twister.
Words are her allies,
Thoughts are the pieces of the puzzle,
She is the *Master Puzzle-Maker.*

Academia

- Academic Arena
- Special Education for Brain Injury
- Environment
- Directing Traffic
- Can Creativity Enhance Cognition?

Academia

Academic development necessitates accommodations to supplement an individual with a disability's learning process. In working with children and adults with TBI, there is a great variety of special needs that may be encountered. When a student is suitably accommodated and feels confident and supported, academic advancement is obtainable! In training to work with children and adults with TBI[v], I learned about the great variety of special needs that may be encountered as well as how to develop their learning skills.

It is important for a person with a head injury (or any other disability) to maintain a good relationship with the Special Educator, Resource Room Teacher or Disability Support Services (DSS). The DSS at George Washington University helped me with one accommodation in particular which really helped me to make it through my studies. This accommodation was the recording of my text on cassettes. It enabled me to listen to my reading assignments on cassette while at the same time, read the material, thus assisting me in being better able to retain the material. The DSS successfully provided the accommodation that I needed in order to succeed.

Overcoming challenges makes a person strong. In their book, Boundaries, Dr. Henry Cloud and Dr. John Townsend (1992) state "When a baby bird is ready to hatch, if you break the egg for the bird, it will die. The bird must peck its own way out of the egg into the world. This aggressive 'workout' strengthens the bird, allowing it to function in the outside world. Robbed of this responsibility, it will die." People as well as birds need certain challenges to strengthen them. For people with disabilities to accomplish challenges, to support or accommodate them will make them more able to succeed; this is what is humane, as well as a legal responsibility!

A person is able to accomplish goals when they set their mind and will to it, even when challenges present themselves. Others should try and help, or at least try not to hinder a survivor from reaching her/his goals. One thing that I do not appreciate, is when others (doctors, professionals, family or acquaintances) underestimate what a person living with a brain injury is capable of doing. To deny a person the opportunity to grow or relearn skills (i.e. break through the egg) does a great disservice to that person's recovery process. A little encouragement and positive feedback can go a long way toward rebuilding self-esteem and life skills, both being crucial in recovery. Sometimes a shift in attitude can open up new doors.

Academic Arena

I sharpen my sword,
Put on my protective armor,
To prepare myself
For the academic arena.
I battle my doubts,
Persevere against other's skepticism,
Psych myself for a victory.

Disability Support Services
Gets me ready for my battles.
Gears me with accommodations,
Educates me about my rights,
I am reinforced
As is needed
In order to make it.

I am hiking up the hill of self-confidence.
Advocacy diminishes the struggle,
Learning with cognitive impairments
Is not an effortless path.
Accommodations ease the way,
We do have to tell teachers what we need,

My problem with memory,
Often makes me think
Graduation I may never see!
I fight those self-doubts,
They keep creeping up.
Perseveration of perseverance,
It takes a willingness
To release bad attitudes,
To work beyond
What I think is my limit,
I keep chugging along...
No matter myself.

Invisible disability -
It's Ok with me,
Is it Ok with you?
Schooling results in forced socializing,
Like it or not.
With an inner eye,
I view the understanding
People have got
- Or have not.

Inclusion
In the school of hard knocks,
Individual Education Plan,
Interventions,
Just because you make a mistake,
Doesn't mean you are a mistake,
Positive feedback.

Keeping the mental sword sharpened,
Persistence,
Commitment,
Hours of study,
Even if it takes
Twice as much effort
As everyone else!

No matter what anybody tells you,
With a brain injury,
Academia isn't an impossible aim,
You just need to stand strong
And know how to play the game!

Special Education for Brain Injury

Consulting,
Listening,
Assessing,
Collaborating,
Strategizing,
Individualizing instruction,
Developing accommodations,
Prescriptive education,
Repetition,
Instructional leading,
Demonstrating,
Modeling,
Making recommendations,
Helping parents, family & friends -
Understand,
Accept,
Adjust their expectations.
Community networking,
Making referrals,
Outreach,
Consulting with administration,
Policies & procedures,
Helping a student transition,
Hospital to school,
Aiding students and family in coping,
Self-discovery,
Facilitating self-confidence,
Repetition,
Life skills coaching,
Behavior modification,

Implementing strategies,
Making remediations,
Did I say repetition?
Teaching about disability rights,
Accommodating whatever –
to help a student learn.

Neuroeducational Specialist

Environment

It may not be so clear,
What influences
may cause disturbances to appear.

There may be a drop
in the student's learning curve,
I want to cue you in
to some things
you might want to observe.

So many influences
can scatter the attention,
Some basic classroom environmental issues,
I just want to mention -

What types of visual aides are being supplied?
Are the students' learning skills fortified?

Is it mostly verbal instruction?
Might the student have trouble
with oral comprehension?

Visually,
How is information presented?
Be aware
of how well it's being attended.

How is the room lit & organized?
Might the classroom
be a bit oversized?

Is adaptive equipment being used?
If so -
How thoroughly to it
has the student been introduced?

How about proximity –
To distracting peers,
windows and the blackboard?
Have any of these influences ever been explored?

How's the noise level in the room?
All of these
could make it difficult
for information to be consumed.

If studies are difficult,
You might want to environmentally assess,
Then you can strategize
to minimize the distress.

Directing Traffic

Special education,
Cerebral evolution,
Life skills rehabilitation,
Develop knowledge,
Strength of will,
Intuition,
A single step forward
Is what puts us on the road,
Heading toward our destination.

If to function is difficult for you -
Doing it your method,
You don't have to stay,
Don't fret,
It's okay,
Adapt and adjust,
Come, try it another way.

Child -
Get that negative self-concept
Out of your head.
Reform that
Which to yourself you've said.
Talk to yourself gently,
Positively instead.
You will accomplish your goals,
Don't be misled.
Go on,
You can do it,
Full speed ahead!

I've learned
To direct others
Along the rehab-road.
Prevent them
From going through overload,
Make sure they don't corrode,
Help them to safely emotionally unload,
Keep them in the rehabilitative mode,
I advocate for them -
Tolerance and integrity
Is what their owed!

Stop and go,
Red light → *STOP!*
I call a halt to:
Drug and alcohol misuse,
Bad attitudes that serve as an excuse,
Tendency to be an out and out recluse,
Allowing inappropriateness to seduce,
Inner battles –
I try to make a truce,
Green light → *GO!*
I direct the group to setting goals,
Break it down even further,
Objectify,
To aid them in gaining control,
I serve as their patrol,
To help them get out of their hellhole.

Personal traffic I direct,
When folks with brain injury do arrive.
Make sure rehab
Doesn't squeeze out the juices
That keep them alive.
Attempt to see to it
That they stay revived!
Bloom new self-concepts,
Smiles flow freely,
We all buzz around our hive,
Socialize,
Everyone learns to live,
Rather than just be alive!

Can Creativity Enhance Cognition?

Promoting Balance with Education

In the learning process, a person utilizes both hemispheres of the brain. The right hemisphere regulates holistic, visual-spatial, and intuitive processes. The left hemisphere governs the linear, verbal-analytical, and logical processes. These functions are continuously collaborating to make up who we are. A comprehensive education includes strengthening and balancing both sides of the personality. The creative arts inter-webbed with cognitive learning can be used as a fundamental catalyst for this kind of balancing. People are more receptive to learning when they are having fun!

Educating solely the right or left hemisphere of the brain would be educating a segregated part of the person. When only analytical or logical functions are utilized in education, learning and perceptual deficits may appear later in students' lives. Similarly, exposing students only to the creative processes would not be a balanced teaching strategy.

We may choose to develop in either a scholarly or artistic manner, or we may come to blend the two. Writing poetry is an example of a tool for a more comprehensive educational experience. It simultaneously exercises verbal, analytical and visual as well as holistic, visual and intuitive processes. The interest in blending creative and cognitive works opens many doorways for exploration and development. Consider great artists and scientists, such as Ludwig van Beethoven, and Albert Einstein; these men acquired a certain degree of holistic/linear or intuitive/analytical balance. True artists or scientists often need to exceed pre-established cultural norms in order to accomplish great works. Cognition simply does not equal the rational mind; it is the combination of the intuitive or holistic processes, and the linear, analytical processes that synthesize and form intellectual genius. Did Albert Einstein formulate the Theory of Relativity by merely analyzing observations and data, or did he use holistic-imaging and his intuitive processes?

Facilitating the artistic process

A teacher who utilizes appropriate strategies and teaching techniques can bring out the untapped genius of students. The instructor serves as a facilitator of the artistic experience; no one can be said to "teach" art. A teacher can train a student in technique only. A piece of art is the outcome of personal inspiration. Whether it is Rembrandt painting a masterpiece, or a child reeking havoc in a scribble drawing, each is personally inspired. A teacher facilitates a student's interests, points out their strengths, encourages their talents to develop and also acts as a model. The teacher exposes the student to the world around him, (e.g. including: observing nature, color, and shape) thus helping to build the intelligence and imagination of the pupil. Everybody has a storehouse of creativity. It is the facilitator's job to help individuals to work with or around obstacles and help that person tap into his or her creative potential.

Self-expression is an inherent personal need and the artistic experience can nurture the student's abilities. Rehabilitative therapists recommend clients to practice hobbies and crafts after an injury to reestablish self-confidence and self-esteem. It is known that tactile activities serve to integrate motor and sensory skills. Additionally, intrinsic to the creative process is incidental learning (i.e. in the process of painting, a child incidentally learns about many relevant or generalized topics). By utilizing this teaching strategy, an instructor can use a student's thirst for art in a manner that will promote more of a hunger for cognitive learning.

Creativity can be used in context. Ideally, teaching could creatively adapt to the student's interests (See www.graymatters4u.com - Research: Motivation / Rehabilitation - Can adapting therapy to the student's interest make a difference?). In this way, a quality instructor can utilize art to help a student develop an inquiring mind, one that is flexible and inquisitive. The student will learn to seek solutions in a creative manner. In learning such an approach, s/he can then take cognitive development to its heights.

Nature's Touch

- Land Lovers – Imagine This
- Ocean Manna
- Sea of Translucence
- Monterey Bay Aquarium Report
- Maggie
- Kayak Trip report
- Nature Heals
- Interspecies Communication
- Shared Adventure
- Eskimo Roll
- Surf Sense
- No Sound Barriers
- Consider This

Nature's Touch

The natural environment can be a healing, settling and grounding influence. Whilst participating in any activity or sport, we can become attuned to our environment; whether it is out on the ocean, in the act of walking, jogging, gardening, even playing golf or sitting in the sun. It is an exercise of awareness, not just the physical body, although exercising the physical certainly helps! When we become aware of our personal interaction with our environment, we open a new sensitivity to people and things around us. We can reap many benefits from attuning our awareness.

My most interactive experiences with nature occur in interacting with the ocean. As a kayaker, when I am out on the water, the sense of peace is inclusive. Sitting down in the kayak, I feel close to the swells, waves, winds, tides and ocean life. I feel a part of all that.

Have you ever felt outside of yourself, and yet fully at home where you are? The only place I have such a supra-natural experience is out on the water. Scanning for marine life and experiencing the joy of their presence brings me outside of myself. At the same time, I feel comforted in the marine environment. It is there I feel myself in unison with nature. It is out on the water where I gain the feeling of being most contented with myself. This is my personal place of healing.

> Kayaking helps me get it all in perspective,
> Aids me in keeping myself somewhat objective,
>
> Being surrounded by the ocean seems to help my insides,
> And it's always fun having a nice wave to catch a ride!

Land Lovers - Imagine This

We put our kayaks in the water,
Slice right through the surf,
A little splash of adventure,
A taste of the ocean,
Smiles,
Looking forward
to time out on the water,
Part of me yearns
for the peace I feel out there.
Effortless meditation...
Swells pass,
Boats rise and fall,
Listen...
We can hear quiet
far into the distance.
Pelican patrol passes overhead.
The seagulls cry -
Goouuhh, Goouhh.
Toward the shore,
the waves gently break.
Ksshhh, Ksshhh, Ksshhhh.
Rise and fall,
Being lulled by marine awareness,

A quiet seal pops his nose out of the water,
He looks over our way,
Back under again,
Distant crows cry out -
Raaauhh, Raaauhh,
Paddling out a little further,
We hear the gentle splash
of the paddles plunging into the water.
Stroking down into the fluid depths,
Each caress gives direction,
In the background,
the ocean rustles,
We catch a glimpse of fins surfacing -
A small pod of dolphins
approach us from down-shore,
They arch up,
Catch a breath,
Dive back down,
We hear them forcefully exhale
as they come to the surface,
Pfouuhh, Pfouuhh, Pfouuhh.
We stop paddling,
So not to scare them off.
Want to see how close they'll come -
About 15 feet away,
Then they go under us,
We're captivated by their grace and beauty.
Blessed by their presence,
They bring an aura of lightness,
We watch them swim away,
~ Refreshing ~

Feeling the fluid stillness,
We listen to the water wrinkle.
From out on the mile marker buoys,
Sea lions can barely be heard,
Oouuhh, Oouuhh, Oouuhh,
Sounds heard through the distance,
Freedom of space clears the mind.
Ocean and sky meet,
Marine refuge.

Monterey Bay, California

Ocean Manna

Dolphins make me strong,
They make me sing all day long,

I can't wait to feel them out there beside me again,
They lift me up like no one else can,

Frolicking, splashing, playing,
Their movement takes me

down into my soul so deep,
Tender fruits inside I reap,

I'm out on the sea where they reside,
Dolphin spirit come alive inside!

sea of translucence

tints and shades
array themselves
into colors.
blended yet discrete,
the vivid display
sedates
the mind's torrid currents.
water, mayim, agua, nuk, wasser,
tinted in aquamarine,
deep –
dark –
storm –
navy –
cerulean –

$\Rightarrow$ **blue.**
home
for the sea creatures,
the colorful rooftop
only hints
at the variety
of inhabitants
in the waters
and on the ocean floor.
purity and elegance
dwell inside.

our imperfect minds
glimpse
the fathomless excellence
of nature's way.
such grace
is savored
in interspecies communication,

**touched upon only briefly,
yet held onto forever.**

In the Indian summer of 2002, Heidi was surf kayaking in the waters of Monterey, California, and was visited by a sea otter. The following two poems are based on a true encounter, also included is a Kayak Trip Report to further articulate this extraordinary experience. This is the Monterey Bay Aquarium's report, which tells the background of that particular otter, "Maggie":

<u>Monterey Bay Aquarium Report</u> [xi]

Maggie, the most recent otter to join the exhibit, was found stranded on a beach in San Simeon State Park (San Luis Obispo County) in February 2001. She was about one week old and weighed just over three pounds.

Aquarium staff released Maggie into the wild in October 2001, but recaptured her in February 2003 after receiving several reports about her interacting with divers, surfers and kayakers. Federal officials agreed with aquarium staff that Maggie should be removed from the wild to prevent injury to herself and to people.

Visitors will be able to easily spot Maggie because she is keeping the orange flipper tags she received when she was returned to the wild. Before an otter is released, it is tagged to help identify the animal when it's tracked in the wild. Her name is derived from "Margie," a fortuneteller in John Steinbeck's novel, <u>The Winter of Our Discontent</u> (1961).

Maggie

The sun brought our ventures
to the shores of the Monterey Bay,
We were gifted with a perfect story
that will make your day,

My paddling partner capsized his boat.
He didn't see that wave,
I tapped my helmet,
"Are you OK?"

He tapped his helmet and turned to see,
"Yeah, but that otter was right on top of me..."

I searched the water -
That otter caught my eye,
Looked intently straight into my core,
Immediately swam right up to me
and climbed aboard!

Jumped right on my boat,
No time to flirt,
With absolute trust,
She snuggled down in the cockpit,
riding my skirt,

She wanted my attention,
oh, so bad,
I think she knew,
that me
she had,
She wanted to play,
Tag along in the surf,
I took her for a ride,
because hey -
it's her turf!

The swells rode us up and down,
she nestled up even closer,
our connection profound.

She'd foresee the waves
that would catch the boat
and take us for a ride,
She'd dive off,
Let me ride it in,
Then swim up to my side,

She'd get back on again,
Climb into my lap
and snuggle in,

There were those on shore pointing at us,
Such an unlikely sight,
But she and I,
together,
Knew it felt right.

Perhaps Channel 7
should have gotten a glimpse of us,
So the public could taste

Maggie's immaculate sense of trust!

On shore,
My paddling partners looked out at us,
It struck them as quite funny,
"Looks like Heidi's found a new surfing buddy!"

Kayak Trip Report [xii]

Three Western Sea Kayakers met at Casa Verde Beach in Monterey to go surfing. Once in the surf, Heidi Lerner went to go check on one of the paddlers when he capsized his boat. She asked him if he was Ok; he said he was fine, but said something about an otter. They started looking around.

When Heidi got eye contact with the otter, it immediately approached her boat. That otter jumped aboard and snuggled into her lap (i.e. in the skirt - what attaches the paddler to the boat). She was awed at how comfortable with her it was. She decided to let the otter stay on the boat with her for a while, as this seemed to be it's chosen preference.

The otter rode atop the boat for some time with her. It would see a wave coming that would take the boat and would dive off - Heidi would ride it in and the otter would swim up to the boat in the soup (i.e. in the whitewater, shoreward of where the waves brake) and hop on again. It was along for the ride! In total, they spent 1 1/2 - 2 hours together.

At one point, the otter began to chew on her skirt. She immediately shook her finger and said, "No!" in a firm voice. It bowed its nose like a guilty dog. It seemed that this otter just needed a MOM!!!!

After this very special surfing extravaganza, Heidi reported this otter and it's tag number to the Monterey Bay Aquarium research department. Karl Mayer, the animal-care coordinator for the seal and otter program, informed her that "it" was a she and she was reported to have approached quite a few surfers and kayakers in Monterey. According to her tag number, the aquarium had raised her since she was orphaned at about two weeks old.

In hoping that she would have more of a chance to adopt wild ways, Maggie was captured and moved to a less frequented Piedras Blancas, near San Simeon. Well, this didn't work out, as she continued to approach the more rare surfers and kayakers in San Simeon as well. The researchers then decided that even there, she was not safe and that she would only be safe, living in the confines of the aquarium. The Monterey Bay Aquarium moved her into their otter exhibit. She was named Maggie and in the exhibit, she joined other otters, Rosa and Mae.

When Heidi first heard that Maggie would be contained in the aquarium, she was saddened, but when she thought about it - Maggie loves people, perhaps this would not just be the safest route, but it may also be good for her. When Heidi visited Maggie in the otter exhibit, she saw that Maggie is kept inside of double glass, which means that she cannot see any of the people all around her who are staring at her. If she could, she'd be checking us all out!!! Now she is stuck within the exhibit - not quite the atmosphere for her to exercise her adventurous and loving character.

Heidi hesitated in writing this trip report, but she decided to put it out for educational purposes. Although she thoroughly enjoyed Maggie's antics in the surf and was deeply touched by interacting with this supposedly wild animal, she discourages kayakers from intruding in the wild lives of animals in the sea. All kayakers/boaters/surfers should realize that we are out there in their turf and we should keep our influence to a minimum. If we contribute to taming the wildlife, we are doing them a great disservice. Help keep the animals wild and you could end up keeping them from harm - or from a fate such as Maggie's, which is to live out her days in the confines of an aquarium exhibit.

This is not saying to hold back love for the sea critters. They are deserving of the deepest love and respect!

Paddle on in peace!

Nature Heals

Out doing what I love one day,
Surf kayaking in Monterey,
I caught eyes with this sea otter,
She came over my way,
Swam up on her own accord,
She didn't hesitate
And climbed aboard!

I repeat –
I didn't approach her,
She approached me,
So nobody can get aghast legally.

This otter stayed on my boat
For two hours!
An intimacy with the wild –
Awakened my own natural child.

Ooohh!!!
When I think of her flawless sense of trust,
My insides just want to combust!

A personal healing,
An indescribable feeling,
Perhaps a "once in a lifetime experience",
One that has enhanced my well-being and confidence!

I paddled out past the surf,
So I could spend quiet time,
Just her and me,
I breathed her in -
Mmmmm...
THE DEPTHS OF THE SEA!

At one point and time,
She wanted to get even closer...
I flung that sweet, furry mass,
Right over my shoulder!
And there she lay,
The nicest fur coat
I ever had on before,
Then again,
She's the only one I ever wore!

You might think
"What does this have to do with brain injury?"
- It's not about what makes me feel bad,
But what makes me grow -
AND SETS ME FREE!

In rehab,
They say it's all about environment.
I'm saying to you -
Reach out in nature,
Take what is sent!
Whether it be in the ocean,
The mountains or in your garden,
The aim is to lighten your heart,
Where it has hardened.

For me,
This experience
Was a gift from the Lord,
- Who knows what I need
To make my insides soar!

Thankful I am
For this natural intimacy,
Which has touched me
With a love and concern
For the mammals of the sea!

Interspecies Communication

It is always such a treat,
When those of different kinds meet,

Even if we only catch it through the visual,
The affect can be quite medicinal,

I want to give you a touch of this delight,
So you can taste the sense of peace it ignites...

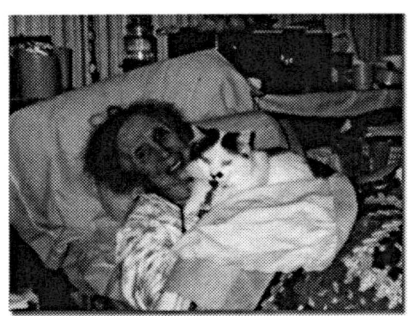

Shared Adventure

It's a **Day on the Beach**[xiii]
In Santa Cruz,
We met waiting to get out onto the water,
You were the boy with the steady grin.,
We started talking,
The budding of a friendship did begin.

Just the idea of going kayaking,
Thrilled you to the bones!
Many served
So you could share this adventure,
They took you from your wheelchair,
Put you in my kayak,
On board,
We went off for a ride...

Shared Adventure -
Pushed by lots of caring hands,
We beat through the surf,
Slithered right through,
Then out on to the calm water,
Feeling the swells,
Rise and fall,
Out there together,
Feeling a little bit of nature,

Aough, Aough, Aough,
The sea lions acknowledge
our presence.
I'll take you for a tour...
Santa Cruz wharf,
- Sea lion community,
Kayak – eye to eye view,
I said -
They'll look you right in the eye!

Back out onto the water's horizon -
Now, we'll go see the surfer's turf -
Cowell's break - good beginner's surf,
Next is Indicators,
Then Steamers Lane,
For the more skilled,
Or the more brave,
The surfers want it that way.

Ocean-side of Steamers,
Seal Rock
Covered by a hoard of sea lions,
...Just chillin'.
They're talking at us -
Aough, Aough, Aough.
I'm happy to share this retreat with you,
This is where I come
To retreat into their world.

Back in - to Cowell's beach,
Other disabled
Waiting to share an adventure!
We pull in through the surf,
Gracefully,
Smoothly,
...I take care of you,
When you're in my boat!

Out there,
I think we developed some trust...
We share a gentle side,
Caring, tolerating, accepting,
As we must!

I'm glad I was able to take you for a ride,
For out on the water,
We converse with our insides.
Shared Adventure for you,
Shared Adventure for me,
It's a special day,
Helping the disabled
Explore the wonders of the sea!

Transfer Hoist - transfers a person from wheelchair into kayak!

A touch of an adventure!

A bit of fun!

Caring hands

Eskimo roll

(Sung to Helter Skelter - the Beatles, 1968)

I go down to the bottom,
I go back
To the top of the tide,
I set up,
And I turn,
And I go for a ride,
And I see -
Can I do it again!
- Do you,
Don't you,
Want it to save you?
Coming down fast,
And don't let it break you!
Tell me,
Tell me,
Tell me the answer,
You may be a paddler,
But you ain't no dancer!

Surf Sense

I am seduced by the ocean's ways,
My lifestyle is pulled closer,
As the sea
I embrace.

I set aside
All that gets me astir,
Just when I hear her LOUD WHISPER.

Sometimes I feel as though
I'm on the edge of the world,
Capturing the mysteries,
Living off
What the sea unfurls.

Through time out on the water,
I learn how to behave,
To read the ocean's signs,
Identify the right waves.

Out on the swells
Is where
I see the beauty...
It helps me to see personal scars
Embedded in my image of me.

It takes a little guts
To be out there
On the sea,
Even more
To take in
What it offers me,

Adventurousness of spirit,
Riding in a fluid
Sense of oneness,
Carving thrills
Into life's monotonous journey!

October 5, 2004

Out on the water again...
Swells coming in,
Scanning the water's horizon
For the right one,
Paddle shoreward,
Catch it,
Steer with my hips,
Shine a moon to the beach,
Leaning up on an edge,
Brace with my paddle,
I carve right down the face.

Again...
Dropping in,
Cutting back,
Rebounding off the white water,
Spin off,
Slice back down the face,
Ride it on in,
Woouuhh!!!!!
Movement,
Freedom,
Freedom of movement,
It's all worth it!
Paddle back out through the breaks,
Once more,
Wait for the right wave.

In the restlessness of myself,
I feel the winds a blowing,
Sometimes I feel
My love for the ocean
Is the thing that keeps me going!

No Sound Barriers

Let us sit and listen to the ocean waves,
In this environment,
I want you to hear what I have to say...

We're all in danger
Of attack on innocent life,
You, me,
All of the animals of the sea!^{xv}

In the marine world,
Hearing promotes survival,
Peace abounds.

Blistering noise debilitates –
- Beware -
INTENSE SONAR SOUND!

Devastating noise,
UNDERWATER TERROR
Slaughter of the innocent,
Disorientation,
Invisible trauma,
Inner injury,
Dying families,
Do we will this?

Used to detect enemy submarines,
Perpetrator:
Low Frequency Active Sonar
U.S. Navy.

Oh Lord -
Do the innocent animals of the sea,
Need to be tortured and slaughtered for our security?

(See Appendix F)

Consider This

Marine jungle,
Aquatic tranquility,
Under-water mammals -
Surviving by sound,
(- use sound to feed, protect themselves &their young,
to mate & keep in community)
ERUPTION OF NATURE,
Earsplitting ocean noise ⇨
Disorientation,
Blood drips inside the skull,
Frying of the temporal lobe.
Distorting the basic functions of the brain,
Traumatic Brain Injury
To the mammals of the sea,
Whales – STRANDED!
Victimized,
DEAD
Definite threat to the survival of the species!

I'm taking this chance,
To let you know,
How this really bothers me!

Being a survivor of a brain injury
And a maiden of the sea,
A marine life advocate
I must be!

The importance of this I must try and convey -
The Marine Mammal Protection Act
We must come to obey!
Not just me and you,
The government too!

Grounds for reflection:
Shaken Baby Syndrome -
Causes a brain injury to an innocent child,
- Illegal!
Low Frequency Active Sonar & Seismic air guns...
Result in trauma to the brain -
To the harmless animals of the sea,
WHERE IS THE MORALITY?
A neglectful attitude,
Abusive behavior,
Is this the American way?

Human generated ocean noise pollution,
Caused by:
- Military sonar,
- Seismic air guns,
Used in oil and gas exploration,
- The shipping industry,
Brings about disorienting background noise,

Seaflow, International Ocean Noise Coalition, NRDC ...
Become the WARRIORS,
To protect the precious,
Innocent life
Under the sea.

**Man-made noise levels underwater double
every decade -**
**Our economic vitality depends on the health of
our oceans!**

Let us become aware
AND COME TO CARE!
Most TBI survivors,
To others
Would never want to likewise impair,
Not wanting another
To know the pain that s/he did forbear.
Come to shout how underwater noise pollution is unfair!
Let your voice be known.
Tell them why you care!

Let's write in and tell them how we feel.
PROTECT THE SEA CREATURES FROM GETTING A RAW DEAL!
(See Appendix F).

Circle of Support

- Josephine
- Mirrors
- Type of Injury
- What Survivors Want in a Support Group
- Greatest Challenge
- Greatest Advantage of Having a Head Injury
- What Can Help a Brain Injury Survivor

Circle of Support

Sometimes you just need a person to listen to you to lift your world. When someone can relate to what you're going through, it truly helps to ease your burdens. Support groups provide a place where people simply know they can be understood. Participants relate to each other, hear one another's experiences and share their concerns; psychological and emotional support is given and received, better attitudes are formulated and everyone leaves feeling more apart of a community. It is very important for brain injury survivors to socialize and communicate. In facilitating groups, I encourage everyone to express him or herself. The purpose of Gray Matters Support Group is not for guest speakers to tell us about brain injury or types of healing, it is a chance for the psychosocial needs of the group to be attended to. The tone of the group remains uplifting.

Gray Matters was initiated at George Washington University as an Intercollegiate Brain Injury Support Group; I continued facilitating groups, after moving to California. I presently facilitate a group that is open to the public, at Scripps Hospital in Southern California. The group is called *Gray Matters – North County Brain Injury Support Group*. This group is the source of personal information for the final five poems. In these poems, I mostly cited what the members in the group had to say. The purpose of this poetry is to show the great variety in people's individual experiences with brain injury. The examples they set speak louder than words.

I acknowledge and thank all members of Gray Matters, both at George Washington University and in North County, San Diego for their enthusiasm and inspiration. In my thanks, I also include the Santa Cruzians in the New Options group. This book is for each of you and you know who you are. Additionally, I thank Josephine for all that she shared with me; I learned from her that healing moves in a circular motion.

Josephine

I would like to introduce you
to Josephine,
She's a woman
I once worked with,
Who taught me
what TRUE CARING means.
A sweet lady -
Who lost her balance,
Fell down the stairs,
Though she didn't want to,
She needed to
accept help with personal repairs.

I'd come in and help her
adapt and cope,
She'd say that I'd cause her
to salvage some hope.
When she'd come upon troubles,
The two of us would strategize,
To avoid her efforts coming to a demise,
We'd individualize,
Then she'd try that on for size.

She remained a proud woman,
In private
her personal affairs were kept.
I'd aid her only
with what she'd accept!

At the same time,
She had other illnesses
going on inside,
She chose not
to get treated by chemo,
This was up to her to decide.

Her kitty she treasured,
Like her little angel,
The two of them seemed to be
intimately entangled.

Her life had been tough,
Her body would always be sore,
Nevertheless...
She'd love
whomever
would come in her door.

But oh, please,
Josephine was not a passive lady
in whose life you could barge,
If she didn't like something,
I'd just watch her take charge!

I cherished
that delicate, fragile lady,
for the inner peace and strength she contained;
And that's observing her with a traumatized brain!

She was a single mother of two
in the time of the Depression,
A counselor in her day -
Now, friends would call on her
for her sweet-hearted intercession.

Together with all of this,
Josephine was a journalist too,
She would say to me,
"There's a lot we share,
between me and you!"

At times I'd be working
with her and her condition,
Out of the blue,
she'd yell out to me
"Don't end a sentence
with a preposition!"

If you looked around her room,
Everything would seem disarrayed.
I dared not move things,
For in her random order,
She knew
where everything laid!

We'd talk and talk,
Because she felt that in me
she could trust,
She'd allow me to proceed
with interventions,
She'd say "If you must!"

She knew of my personal struggle
with injury to the head,
This really helped her,
as she continually said.

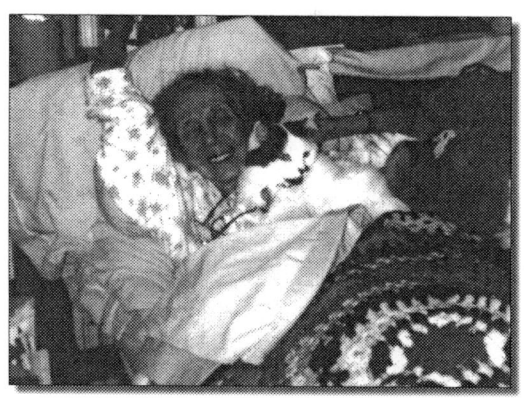

Life skills,
Organization,
Memory improvement,
We'd work into our regime.
She'd say I helped her
avoid depression
and to keep her self-esteem.

After working with Josephine
for nearly a year,
We had the chance
to really get to know each other,
Our hearts,
We both came to endear.

She'd always keep me guessing,
She was one of a kind.
...It's when I fully appreciated her,
She'd allow me to enhance
her troubled mind.

When it was close friends
she was among,
She'd like to go by "Josie",
As this would make her feel young.

An elderly woman,
This we could all see,
But don't be beguiled,
Sometimes she'd be as playful
as a little child!

I was there
to be of service to her,
And I would leave her place
feeling afreshed,
Angel of a lady -
In helping her,
I'd come out feeling blessed!

Mirrors

Put your hands into the circle,
You will be reached back out to.
Circular support

We all get caught up in
What's going on in our world,
In the circle,
The spotlight is taken off of ourselves.

We get a chance to -
Objectify,
Clarify,
Something of significance is sought,
Personal reflections are caught,

Our broken mirrors -
Reflect remnants of each other,
Those resemblances help us
Get to know ourselves better.

Everyone gets time to speak...
Express
Or repress,
The feather is passed,
We come to really listen to one another,

Zero in and...
Mirrors reflect mirrors,
Showing multiple dimensions,
Metacognitive bathing,

Light sees the light,
Edify,
Fortify,
Simplify,
On the circle we come to rely,
We are all an intrinsic piece of the pie.

Type of Injury

Car wreck,
Went flying through the windshield
with a nasty landing,
Shot in the head (Open Head Injury)[xvi],
Riding my bike -
A dog ran in front,
Hemorrhage in the Brain Stem (Acquired),
Head on motorcycle collision,
Rolled car in avoiding other car,
Fell from horse onto lava rock,
An aneurysm went off
when being operated on.
(Acquired → Iatrogenic),[xvii]
Strokes (Acquired),
Pulmonary Embolism (Block in lung – Genetic),
Ran off the road by drunken driver,
Schizophrenic – been hallucinating since young,
-Treated with shock therapy (Iatrogenic),
Open Heart Surgery led to a Stroke (another Iatrogenic).
Brain Aneurysm (Acquired),
Motorcycle wreck → Anoxia,
Another hospital mishap
due to neglect of the nurses (Traumatic → Iatrogenic),
Hematoma to the right frontal cortex (Acquired),
In a motorcycle accident,
Suffered Spinal Chord and Traumatic Brain Injury.

(All head injuries listed here are Traumatic, unless otherwise noted.)

What Survivors Want in a Support Group

"Fellowship,
People that can relate
to what I've been through,
Social support,
I am always looking to help others out...
A place I can feel safe,
Compatibility,
To feel secure enough
with the group
that we can feed off
each other's hope & strength.
Not being judged,
My growth is recognized,
To gather with people
who know I'm perfect (!),[xviii]
To develop new friends
(- As "friends" rapidly diminished after my accident),
To find out how everyone else
deals with their problems,
We all get stuck in our own lives.
We feel we're alone and isolated,
- but we're not!
To feel everyone else's difficulties
sure makes me grateful for what I've got!

I want to be around others
who understand what I'm going through,
Community,
We see one another as we are.
We're not looking to take anything
from each other.
I get overwhelmed easily -
I get a lot out of it.
Feel like I'm part of something,
Networking,

If life gives you lemons,
MAKE LEMONADE!

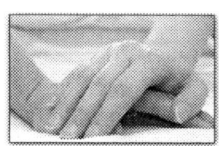

I am better off
with a supportive group of people,
To be free of criticism,
Acceptance, Appreciation, & Affection,
I'm always sitting off in the corner.
Holding back to myself,
Withdrawn,
I want to receive
some of the support I need -
I'm just starting
to ask for help.

My spouse and friends have deserted me -
I'm looking to build self-esteem back.
METAMORPHOSIS...
~ Like a butterfly ~
You get your wings.

Like a colony of bees...
Pollinate, Protect & Provide,
If one goes astray,
The group sends out signals
to locate the bee in turmoil.

To have some fun –
Bounce stuff off of each other,
To be part of a think tank,
Brain injured - brainstorming,
(Watch out!)

We communicate
for optimal survival.
The bees tell each other
where the flowers are!
Acquaintances
grow into friends.

**It's better to light a candle,
than to curse the darkness!"**

That's what we're all looking for.

Greatest Challenge

Taking better care of myself,
Thinking before I act,
Not acting off the cuff,
Making my own decisions,
Losing my orientation,
Having no idea where I'm going in the car,
Losing my train of thought,
I'll be going somewhere
and forget where I'm going.
I don't have anything that is a challenge for me -
because I have accepted my difficulties.
My family accepting me for who I am,
Getting to know people again,
Coming to know who my friends are
and who are not my friends
(i.e. Knowing who are my allies),
I can't talk, move or write as well as I used to,

but it's Ok, "I'm perfect (!)"[xviii]
Not becoming dependent on medication,
Keeping my SANITY,
Serenity, Acceptance, New hope, Integrity, Trust, Yahweh,
(or the highway),
Getting acceptance from others,
Accepting myself,
Mobility,
When doctors told me I'd never walk again,
- They never told me I wouldn't fly!!!
"Do you pollinate?"
(i.e. Pollination causes crossbreeding)

Having scattered attention,
Finding my way in unfamiliar territories,
Not comparing myself to how I was in the past,
Accepting where I'm at now.

Greatest Advantage of Having a Head Injury

I'M FINDING A NEW NORMAL!
It brought me closer to my family,
Learned to work on the computer,
Developed my skills in writing,
Disability parking (!),
It's given me a chance
to know myself better.
I used to never know
when I got upset,
Now I get to be human.
My wife keeps me on the right track,
She is my greatest advantage.
Coming to know my true strengths,
The pendulum swung to the other side -
I used to be a womanizing drunk,
Now, I am more caring
about relationships.
My leg was saved from amputation,
I got to retire at 39,
After my injury,
I lost my wife...
The rest is easy,
This gave me a push to go on,
I became a fighter
against the odds,
I won't give up –
I got strong,
Motivated,
Empowered!

I came to appreciate
my family more...
They're looking out for me.
I live more and love deeper.

What Can Help a Brain Injury Survivor?

Know and accept my limitations,
Be more understanding,
Not make knee-jerk assumptions
about why a person behaves as they do,
Assume that I can handle my work,
Unless proven otherwise,
The law needs to change -
To protect a person from losing
their financial assets
when they're in a vulnerable state.

Come over and do my laundry (!)[xviii]
Leave me time to help myself,
Survivor's husband says:
Have more patience -
People get frustrated
when she doesn't live up to
how she was.
Not be judgmental
or set expectations,
Encourage me to be easier on myself,
Come more from the heart,
Look at me as a striver and a survivor❣

Glossary

Acquired Brain Injury – An injury to the brain that has occurred since birth. It can be caused by an external physical force or by an internal occurrence. The term acquired brain injury refers to both traumatic brain injuries, such as open or closed head injuries and non-traumatic brain injuries, such as strokes, and other vascular accidents, infectious diseases (e.g. encephalitis, meningitis), anoxic injuries (e.g. hanging, near drowning, choking, anesthetic accidents and severe blood loss), metabolic disorders, (e.g. insulin shock, liver and kidney disease), and toxic products taken into the body through inhalation or ingestion. The term does not refer to brain injuries that are congenital or brain injuries induced by birth trauma.

Acquired brain injury may result in mild, moderate or severe impairments in one or more areas, including cognition; speech-language communication; memory; attention and concentration; reasoning; abstract thinking; problem solving; sensory, perceptual and motor abilities; psychosocial behavior; physical functions; and information processing (Savage & Wolcott, 1994).

Acute Rehabilitation – The early phase of rehabilitation, which usually begins when a person becomes medically stable. The program is designed to be comprehensive and based in a medical facility with a typical length of stay of 2-3 months.

Aphasia – Loss of the ability to express oneself (Expressive Aphasia) and/or to understand language (Receptive Aphasia). Aphasia is caused by damage to brain cells rather than deficits in speech or hearing organs.

Blast Brain Injury - Results from the pressure wave generated by an explosion (i.e. hand grenades, suicide /terrorist bombings—see Hands of Mercy in Online References). Primary blast injuries occur from an interaction with the over-pressurized, explosive wave; secondary blast injuries can also occur by other means such as impact from blast-energized debris, the individual being physically thrown, burns and/or inhalation of gases and vapors. Statistics are not clear, but the percentage of blast attacks resulting in head injuries are significantly high.

Closed Brain Injury – Occurs when the head accelerates and rapidly decelerates or collides with another object (for example, a windshield of a car) and brain tissue is damaged, not by the presence of a foreign object within the brain, but by a violent smashing, stretching and twisting of brain tissue. Closed brain injury typically causes diffuse tissue damage (i.e. all over the brain) that results in a disability, which is generalized and highly variable.

Coma – A state of unconsciousness from which a person cannot be aroused, even by powerful stimulation, there is lack of response. Eyes are typically closed; there are no sleep/wake cycles.

Executive functions – Planning, prioritizing, organizing, problem solving, sequencing, self-monitoring, self-correcting, inhibiting, initiating, controlling or altering behavior. Also referred to as "higher level functions".

Hemisphere – Either of the two symmetrical halves of the cerebrum.

> **Right** – Damage to this area can cause visual-spatial deficits (e.g. the person may have difficulty following directions or have a bad sense of direction).
>
> **Left** – Damage to this area may disrupt a person's ability to understand spoken and/or written language.

Iatrogenic – Describes a symptom or illness brought on unintentionally by something that a doctor does or says.

Lobes –

> **Frontal** - Front part of the brain; involved in executive skills, attention, personality and a variety of higher cognitive functions.
>
> **Occipital** – Region in the back of the brain that processes visual information. Damage to this lobe can cause visual deficits.
>
> **Parietal** – Located behind the frontal lobe at the top of the brain. The two sides of this lobe of the brain have distinct functions.

Temporal – Located at about the level of the ears. Also sectioned off into two lobes, these lobes allow a person to tell one smell from another and one sound from another. They also help in sorting new information and are believed to be responsible for short-term memory.

Metacognitive - a survivor's awareness of his/her own knowledge and skills.

Open Head Injury – Injuries resulting in a penetrating wound to the brain.

Post-Traumatic Amnesia – A period of hours, weeks, days or months after the injury when a person exhibits a loss of day-to-day memory. The person is unable to store new information and therefore has a decreased ability to learn. Memory of this period is never stored; therefore things that happened during this period cannot be recalled.

Post-Traumatic Stress - An anxiety disorder that develops in many individuals who have had major traumatic experiences. The person is typically numb at first but later has symptoms including flashbacks to the traumatic scene, depression, excessive irritability, guilt (for having survived while others may have died), recurrent nightmares, and overreactions to sudden noises (Medicine.net, 1996-2005).

Psychosocial skills – Refers to the individual's adjustment to the injury (and resulting disability) and one's ability to relate to others. Includes feelings about self, sexuality and the resulting behaviors.

Memory

Autobiographical is memory for the people, places, objects, events, and feelings that go into the story of your life, (White Gloves: How We Create Ourselves Through Memory, John Kotre)

Episodic is experience based. This would include memories of events and occurances. It is enhanced by sensory input such as sights, sounds, music, smells and touch. Many times episodic memories are triggered by emotions put on the I recollectiontion. (CrossRoadsInstitute.org)

Long-term is divided into three parts: Episodic, Semantic and Procedural memory. It resides in the deep unconscious and can be viewed as the "repository" of all our knowledge. (CrossRoadsInstitute.org)

Procedural is hands on learning. When we learn a skill such as riding a bike or playing a sport, motor memory is necessary. These skills can only be learned by physically doing them. It is automatic memory. (CrossRoadsInstitute.org)

Prospective is memory to complete future tasks, such as recalling to give a note to someone when you next see them, pick up milk on the way home, or remembering to keep an appointment (National Institute of Health, ClinicalTrials.gov).

Semantic would include remembering specific information such as text books information, math, names, facts and figures. (CrossRoadsInstitute.org)

Short-term refers to the bits of information we can hold in our head at any given time and lasts between 1 second and 24 hours depending upon how much importance you put on the information. You would use this type of memory for phone numbers and zip codes. (CrossRoadsInstitute.org)

Neuropsychology – The scientific study of the relationship between the brain and mental life or the study of brain-behavior relationships.

Rehabilitation (i.e. Rehab) The providing of training, therapy or other types of help to somebody who has survived a serious injury (illness or addiction), that will enable him or her to live a healthy and productive life.

Seasonal Affective Disorder (i.e. S.A.D.) – An affective syndrome characterized by emotional episodes (depression being the most relevant for brain injury) recurring regularly during seasons of the year. Although research is still being conducted on this disorder, it has been found that significant change in environmental light does have an affect on modifying melatonin secretion, which is responsible for SAD. (Beaumont, Kenealy & Rogers. 1996).

Sequelae – A condition as a consequence of an injury.

Support Group – A group established for persons with disabilities and/or families to discuss the problems they may be having in coping with their life situation, to seek solutions to these problems and to provide social support.

Traumatic Brain Injury – Damage to living brain tissue caused by an external, mechanical force. It is usually characterized by a period of altered consciousness (amnesia, coma) that can be very brief or very long. Orthopedic, visual, aural, neurological, perceptive, cognitive or emotional impairments may result. The term does not include brain injuries that are caused by insufficient blood supply, toxic substances, malignancy, disease producing organisms, congenital disorders, birth trauma or degenerative processes.

Definitions are taken from these resources:

Savage, Ronald C. & Wolcott, Gary F. (Editors). (1995). An Educator's Manual -What educators need to know about brain injury. Washington DC: Brain Injury Association, Inc.

Savage, Ronald & Wolcott, Gary F. (Editors) (1994). Educational Dimensions of Acquired Brain Injury, Austin, Texas: Pro-ed.

Encarta World English Dictionary, Macintosh, 2004.

Other sources are listed beside the definitions.

Appendix

A. I want to explain why it is that I spell "God", G-d. The third command-ment states "Thou shall not take the Lord's name in vain" (Deuteronomy 5:11), thus it is a Jewish tradition to not fully spell out the name of the Lord. Additionally, in Leviticus it says "You shall not profane My holy Name; rather I should be sanctified by the Children of Israel. I the Lord who sanctifies you." (Leviticus 22:32).

B. The George Washington University Brain Injury Programs

The George Washington University (GW), in Washington D.C., offers graduate programs for people who want to teach or help people with brain injuries. In addition to this very unique professional training, GW also started a Center for research and special projects. It is called the Center for Education and Human Services in Acquired Brain Injury. The Center and it's programs are dedicated to helping professionals who work with people with brain injuries better understand what a person with a brain injury needs.

The goals of the Center for Education and Human Services in Acquired Brain Injury (CEHSABI) are to conduct applied research and implement special projects that will help to increase the quantity and quality of education and training for professionals who can help to improve the lives of people with brain injuries and their families. The center offers a master's degree (MA), an educational specialist degree (EdS), and a graduate certificate program in transition special education and brain injury.

CEHSABI has newly developed a 15 credit hour distance learning Graduate Certificate Program in special education, transition, and brain injury that can be obtained online. This certificate supplements and enhances the knowledge base of another degree. These programs at GW are pioneers in providing professional preparation at the graduate level for brain injury (for contact information, see Online Refereces).

C. Common Psychosocial Problems Following Brain Injury

Acts immature for age
Has inappropriate manners and mannerisms
Cannot understand humor and "size up" situations
Gets frustrated easily
Cannot inhibit inappropriate behaviors (disinhibition)
Is inappropriately affectionate toward others
Cannot see others' viewpoint (egocentricity)
Has limited insight into own abilities and behaviors
Cannot correct behavior after feedback
Gets stuck on one thought or behavior
Appears apathetic or poorly motivated
Takes too many risks or acts impulsively
Acts fearful
Gets angry out of proportion to cause
Is verbally and/or physically aggressive
Appears anxious or depressed
Changes mood rapidly
Laughs or cries for no apparent reason
Isolates self
Seeks attention, even with negative behaviors
Is demanding

Is irritable
Gets tired easily
Denies problems
Seems unmotivated and passive.
(Savage &Wolcott, 1994, p. 241)

D. Temperomandibular/Trigeminal Dysfunction

Orthopedic complications of the temperomandibular joint (TMJ) are well recognized and compensatory or cushioning devices are commonly utilized. It is less understood that due to the trigeminal nerve complex located behind the ear, temperomandibular dysfunction can not only cause tightness in the jaw and clenching of the teeth, but also dystrophy in other parts of the body. This neurological rebounding alters patterns of blood flow in the tissues, triggers pain or postural imbalances in certain areas and adversely affects the gait.

The trigeminal complex is the moderator of messages from the body to the brain and the brain to the body. It can interrupt or magnify messages sent through the spinal column. The TMJ complex is neurologically linked to the system of communication between the vertebrae of the spine; the trigeminal nerve connects with the inner ear, hence compression of this nerve cluster does cause problems with balance. Please note that the temperomandibular joint and the trigeminal nerve are close to each other and are mutually provocative.

In the event of a head injury, indirect trauma results from the head being thrust forward (as well as the whole body) while the muscles stay rigidly attached to the mandible. The heavy cranium keeps moving like a cannon ball while the jaw remains anchored to the sternum and shoulder complex by it's insertions.

The tissue becomes permanently injured; the scarred tissue is healed and left in a shortened position.

It is no secret that improper structure leads to improper function. The normal curve in the neck can become flattened during a serious head or neck injury, causing a stretching of the brainstem, much like stretching a banana end to end. When the function of the brainstem is compromised, so is the patient's health. Symptoms that result from such an injury often include dizziness, tinnitus, blurred vision, neck tension, and headaches. Because of their proximity, it is not uncommon for neuromuscular imbalances to occur simultaneously in both the tempero-mandibular joint and upper cervical spine after such an injury (Pietrek, James - Cervical Chiropractor, 2005).

It is important to note that a large portion of the neurological input to the brain goes through the face, mouth and temperomandibular region and over one hundred muscles act in pivoting the jaw during mandibular motion (e.g. chewing or speaking). The sensory and proprioceptive nerves to the brain coming from the jaw's motion set the pattern for a large portion of the motor muscles in the body particularly in the neck, pectoral muscle area of the chest and pelvic region of the spine.

Oral appliances (Kloeffler, G. D., San Diego, 2005) are individually designed to result in craniomandibular decompression and repositioning. This can be understood as alleviating the irritation of the trigeminal nerve by repositioning the jaw. This plan is tentatively aimed at normalizing the neuromuscular dynamics of the rest of the body.

E. Mapping the Brain and Brain Injury
-Brain Injury Association of America webpage

Brain Injury is unpredictable in its consequences.

Brain Injury effects who we are, the way we think, act and feel. It can change everything about us in a matter of seconds. The most important things to remember are:

- * A person with a brain injury is a person first.
- * No two brain injuries are exactly the same.
- * The effects of a brain injury are complex and can vary greatly from person to person.
- * The effects of a brain injury depend on many factors, including cause, location, severity, age of the person, etc..

A Healthy Brain

Before we can understand what happens when a brain is injured, we must realize what a healthy brain is made of and what it does. The brain is enclosed inside the skull. The skull acts as a protective covering for the soft brain. The brain is made of neurons (nerve cells). The neurons form tracts that route throughout the brain as well as the body. These nerve tracts carry messages to various parts of the brain. The brain uses these messages to perform functions. The functions include our thought processes, physical movements, personality changes, behavioral changes, and sensing and interpreting our environment. Each part of the brain serves a specific function and links with other parts of the brain to form more complex functions.

Functions of the Brain:

The brain is divided into main functional sections called lobes. These sections or brain lobes are called the Frontal Lobe, Temporal Lobe, Parietal Lobe, Occipital Lobe. The Cerebellum, and the Brain Stem are also significant portions regarding functions of the brain. Each has a specific function, as described below.

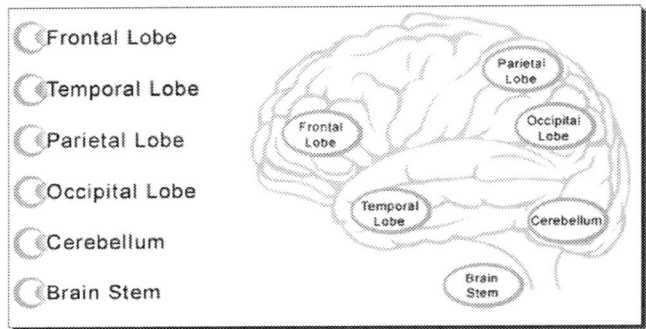

Frontal Lobe

* Problem Solving
* Awareness of abilities and limitations
* Judgment
* Organization
* Inhibition of behavior
* Attention and concentration
* Planning and anticipation
* Mental flexibility
* Self-monitoring
* Ability to control emotion
* Motor Planning
* Changes in personality
* Assigning priorities
* Initiation
* Making decisions
* Interacting socially (Restak, 1991)
* Capability to synthesize signals from the environment

Temporal Lobe
* Memory
* Hearing
* Organization
* Sequencing
* Understanding language (receptive language)

Parietal Lobe
* Sense of touch
* Differentiation (identification - of size, shapes, and colors)
* Spatial perception
* Visual perception

Occipital Lobe
* Vision

Cerebellum
* Balance
* Coordination
* Skilled motor activity

Brain Stem
* Breathing
* Heart rate
* Arousal and consciousness
* Sleep and wake cycles
* Attention and concentration

An Injured Brain:

When a brain injury occurs, the functions of the neurons, nerve tracts, or sections of the brain can be affected. If the neurons and nerve tracts are influenced, they can be unable or have difficulty carrying the messages that tell the brain what to do. This can result in changes in thinking, physical changes, as well as personality and behavioral changes. These alterations can be temporary or permanent. They may cause impairment or a complete inability to perform a function. Some possible changes are described in the following lists.

Thinking Changes
* Memory
* Decision-making
* Planning
* Sequencing
* Judgment
* Attention
* Communication
* Reading and writing skills
* Problem solving skills
* Organization
* Self-perception
* Perception
* Thought flexibility
* Safety awareness
* New learning
* Thought processing speed

Physical Changes
* Muscle movement
* Muscle coordination
* Sleep
* Hearing
* Vision
* Taste
* Smell
* Touch

Personality and Behavioral Changes
* Social skills
* Depression
* Anxiety
* Frustration
* Stress
* Denial
* Self-centeredness
* Anger management
* Coping skills
* Self-monitoring remarks or actions
* Motivation
* Irritability or agitation
* Emotional control & mood swings
* Appropriateness of behavior
* Reduced self-esteem
* Excessive laughing or crying
* Sexual functioning
* Fatigue
* Weakness
* Balance
* Speech
* Seizures

Right or Left Brain

The functional sections or lobes of the brain are also divided into right and left sides. The right side and the left side of the brain are responsible for different functions. General patterns of dysfunction can occur if an injury is on the right or left side of the brain.

Injuries of the Right Side of Brain can cause:
* Visual-spatial impairment
* Visual memory deficits
* Left neglect (inattention to the left side of the body)
* Decreased awareness of deficits
* Altered creativity and music perception
* Loss of "the big picture" type of thinking
* Decreased control over left-sided body movements

Left Side of the Brain
* Difficulties in understanding language (receptive language)
* Difficulties in speaking or verbal output (expressive language)
* Catastrophic reactions (depression, anxiety)
* Verbal memory deficits
* Impaired logic
* Sequencing difficulties
* Decreased control over right-sided body movements

Diffuse Brain Injury
(the injury is throughout the brain)
* Reduced thinking speed
* Confusion
* Reduced attention and concentration
* Fatigue
* Impaired cognitive (thinking) skills in all areas

F. Defending the Silence of the Seas

"Imagine you are walking downtown with the two kids in tow. It's Saturday afternoon. The streets are bustling with people. Suddenly, The Noise, louder than anything you've ever heard, blasts your attention. It sounds like the pulsing pressure of a motorcycle, grating like a car alarm, with the intensity of a foghorn blasting right into your ears. What the? It's so LOUD! Gotta get away. Where is it coming from? People on the street are running every which way, hands glued to their ears, eyes squinting with pain. Not that way. Not there. Try inside the building. Where's Susie? You look down at her terrified face. Blood is trickling from her ears. Her eyes are about to explode. You can't bend down to carry her because your hands are locked over your ears. It doesn't help. The Noise is blaring inside your head. You head into the building. The pulsing. The grating. Machine guns are shooting into your ears. People are falling over each other. You can't hear their screams. You only feel the pulsing pain. And the warm blood running down your neck.

A horror something like this happens to the intelligent animals that live in the sea, whales and dolphins, when the U.S. Navy activates its hyper-loud, under-water sound blaster called Surveillance Towed Array Sensor System (SURTASS) Low Frequency Active (LFA) sonar. The Navy's LFA sonar blasts The Noise so loudly that whale's eardrums break, their sinuses explode, blood hemorrhages in their brains and lungs. In March, 2000, immediately after a Navy LFA sonar test in the Bahamas, fourteen whales ended up "stranded"; their dead bodies washed up on the sand. Biologists from the Woods Hole Oceanographic Institute examined them and observed the tissue damage. The Navy's test blared The Noise at 195 decibels (dB). LFA sonar's full operating volume of 240 dB is 20,000 times LOUDER.

Under the sea, sunlight dims quickly. Deeper than 100 ft., little can be seen. Whales and dolphins use sound to find food, to evade danger, to watch over their young, to communicate with their mates, and to keep their group together as they swim on their migrations. Their sense of hearing is highly developed and very sensitive. They can hear much better than humans, and like bats, they use sound echoes to locate prey and each other. While we use sight to orient ourselves, to know where we are and to communicate, whales and dolphins use hearing. Caught within the radius of The Noise, sea mammals get disoriented. They can't hear, they can't see, they don't know where they are, or which way is up (a well documented symptom of brain injury). They loose their young. Those not killed from tissue damage starve from deafness." (Joffe, Bruce - GIS.Consultants@joffes.com, March 4th, 2005).

Military sonar is only one form of ocean noise pollution; seismic air guns – used in oil and gas exploration and shipping traffic form a racket in the formerly quiet ocean depths. Federal Judge James Larson noted that the U.S. Navy considers sounds above 180 decibels to be potentially harmful to marine mammals (Gaudette, Karen 2002, October 28). Human ear damage occurs at 85 decibels. A congressional inquiry was told by the US Navy in 2001, that an air gun, which gives off 230 decibel piercing blasts, is one of the loudest non-explosive man-made noise in the ocean (sonar emits 235-decibel-plus screeches) (Darby, Andrew 2003, December 6). The background noise in the oceans increased roughly 15 decibels between 1948 and 1998 as the result of an increase in shipping of 465-million-tons, according to "Ocean Noise and Marine Mammals," published by the National Research Council (McElveen, Ryan 2005, April 22) – *all of the references listed here were found on Seaflow's website.*

The man-made underwater noise level has doubled every decade for the past sixty years. Organizations that protect the ocean (NRDC, Seaflow, Earth Island Institute to name a few) want the Navy to use more fish/mammal sensitive sonars, the oil and gas companies to use their exploration guns only when they're sure that no pods of dolphins or whales are around, and that ships are fitted with quieter engines, They additionally want some areas to be declared marine sanctuaries where all human activity is banned.

Ocean noise pollution is a proliferating and serious problem threatening the survival of various cetacean species and fish stocks. Indeed, fish and cetaceans survive by clustering in tight patterns, called schools or pods. They recognize their position in the school by sensing the vibrations of the others through sensors on their skin. Hyper loud sonar effectively "blinds" them from "seeing" each other. Our seafood supply is put in jeopardy by such sonic disruption. Seaflow is an educational nonprofit organization dedicated to protecting whales, dolphins and all marine life from active sonars and other lethal ocean noise pollution. Their website is http://www.seaflow.org. This site has current information on ocean noise issues, relevant articles and news of upcoming events and how you can get involved. For other contact information, see Online References,

How can you help?

- Get educated at Seaflow's website.

- Talk to your family, friends and neighbors or write a letter to the editor about high intensity sonar and the dangers of ocean noise pollution.

- Write to the president and your congressional representatives urging them to oppose deployment of high intensity sonar. You can find out how to contact your President, Vice-President, Senator; find out who your Congressional representative is and how to contact her/him at this web site: http://www.firstgov.com/Contact.shtml

On the next page is a letter that you can zerox and send off to the appropriate authorities. Space was left between the second and third paragraphs so that you can write your personal feelings why you think using sonar in the oceans is not right. I think the authorities need to hear from people who have experienced brain injury or those that know about brain injury and think that causing such harm to marine life is unacceptable. I think they need to be explained exactly why you think that this supposed federal protection is destroying a precious part of our country and the world's oceans.

Date

Dear   :

I write to you in opposition to the deployment of high intensity sonars by the United States Navy. The extreme dangers to marine life are evident and far outweigh any benefit of using these sonars. There are more benign alternatives to many of the high intensity sonars currently in use and in development. Please use your position to deny any funding to this program.

Our environmental laws were enacted in part to protect our marine resources. It is unconscionable that the Navy has been given permission to torture and kill marine mammals. Call an end to this under-water abuse! Please do what you can to defund high intensity sonars in the Defense Appropriations Bill, or work to pass legislation to limit use of these dangerous sonars.

I have strong feelings about how high intensity sonar injures sea mammals and other sea life –

State your feelings here

A healthy global environment is necessary for national security. Please demonstrate that you care about our environment. Please do not support high intensity sonars.

Thank you for your attention regarding this issue,

Sincerely,

Name and address

Bibliography

Beaumont, J. Graham & Kenealy, Pamela M. & Rogers, Marcus J.C. (1996) <u>The Blackwell Dictionary of Neuropsychology</u>, Cambridge, Massachusetts: Blackwell.

Calvin, William H. & Ojemann, George A. (1996) <u>Conversations with Neil's Brain – The Nature of Thought and Language</u>, United States of America: Addison-Wesley.

Cloud, Henry Dr., Townsend, John Dr. (1992) <u>Boundaries</u>, Grand Rapids, Michigan: Zondervan.

Deaton, Ann V., Waaland, Pamela, (1994) Psychosocial Effects of Acquired Brain Injury. In Savage, Ronald C. & Wolcott, Gary F. (Editors), <u>Educational Dimensions of Acquired Brain Injury</u> (Chapter 7, pp 239-255). Austin, Texas: Pro-ed.

Goldberg, Stephen M.D. (1995) <u>CLINICAL NEUROANATOMY - Made Ridiculously Simple</u>, Miami, Florida: Medmaster.

Goleman, Daniel, Ph.D., (1995) <u>Emotional Intelligence</u>, United States of America: Bantam.

Hannaford, Carla PhD. (1995) <u>Smart Moves – Why Learning is not all in your Head</u>, Arlington, Virginia: Great Ocean.

Huxley, Aldous, (1933). <u>Texts and Pretexts: An Anthology of Commentaries</u>, London: Chatto & Windus / New York: Harper & Brothers.

Joffe, Bruce, Geographic Information System Professional (2005, March 4). Defending the Silence of the Seas, <u>Berkeley Daily Planet</u>.

Keyes, Ken Jr., (1985) <u>The Hundredth Monkey</u>, Coos Bay, Oregon: Vision Books.

Kloeffler, G. Davis D.D.S., Personal reference, (2005) San Diego, California.

Lehr, Ellen Ph.D. (1990). <u>Psychological Management of Traumatic Brain Injuries in Children and Adolescents</u>, Rockville, Maryland: Aspen.

Maszak, Marianne Szegedy, April 2004. Driven to Distraction, <u>U.S. News and World Report</u>, 136, (14), 52-62.

National Resource Defense Council. (June 1, 2005). Evidence Showing Harm to Whales Withheld by Bush Administration.

Pietrek, James D.C., Upper Cervical Specialist – NUCCA, Personal reference, San Diego, California (2005).

Pilates, Joeph H., Miller, William J. (Original-1945, Edited-1998) <u>PILATES' – Return to Life Through Contrology</u>, Presentation Dynamics Inc.

Pilates, Joseph H., Miller (Original 1934, Edited-1998) <u>YOUR HEALTH-A Corrective system of excercising that revolutionizes the entire field of physical education,</u> Presentation Dynamics Inc.

Reader - anonymous, (2003).

Savage, Ronald C. & Wolcott, Gary F. (Editors). (1995). <u>An Educator's Manual - What educators need to know about brain injury</u>. Washington DC: Brain Injury Association, Inc. (Glossary).

Savage, Ronald & Wolcott, Gary F. (Editors) (1994). <u>Educational Dimensions of Acquired Brain Injury</u>, Austin, Texas: Pro-ed.

Schulz, Charles M. (2002). <u>The World According to Lucy</u>, Ballantine.

Steinbeck, John (1961). <u>The Winter of our Miscontent</u>, Penguin 20th Century Classics.

Wood, Clement (1992) <u>The Complete Rhyming Dictionary</u>, New York: Bantam Doubleday Dell (This poet's best friend).

Musical References

1. Loggins, Kenny (1991). Conviction of the Heart. On <u>Conviction of the Heart</u>, Columbia.

2. Mitchell, Joni (1970). Big Yellow Taxi. On <u>Ladies of the Canyon</u>, Warner Brothers.

3. Beatles (1968). Helter Skelter. <u>The Beatles (White Album)</u>, Capitol.

Online References

Brain Injury Association of America –
Creating a better future through brain injury prevention, research, education and advocacy (See Appendix E).
http://www.biausa.org

Brain Injury Helpline
familyhelpline@biausa.org. or 1-800-444-6443

Locate state brain injury resources –
http://www.biausa.org/Pages/state_contacts.html.

Death by Medicine Life Extension Magazine,
http://www.lef.org/magazine/mag2004/mar2004_awsi_death_01.htm
Shocking statistics of reported iatrogenic illnesses or injuries brought on unintentionally by doctors.

George Washington University Acquired Brain Injury Program
http://www.gwu.edu/~abictr/ George Washington University offers the ONLY professional preparation degree programs in the country in brain injury! For information on these graduate level programs, e-mail: abictr@gwu.edu or call (202) 973-1032.

Gray Matters
http://www.graymatters4u.com
For additional information and discussion about this book and the author, as well as for personal brain injury rehab services. You can also order copies of the book (autographed if requested) directly from the author.

Monterey Bay Aquarium sea otter exhibit –

http://www.mbayaq.org/efc/efc_otter/otter_cam.asp

Contains a lot of information about otter and other marine-life; it also includes a web-cam of the otters in the exhibit- Mae, Rosa and Maggie.

Seaflow

http://www.seaflow.org

An educational nonprofit organization building an international movement dedicated to protecting whales, dolphins and all marine life from active sonars and other lethal noise pollution. They draw on science, creative action, the arts and community for inspired participation to safeguard the ocean's web of life.

<< Phone: (415) 454-4443   info@seaflow.org >>
1062 Ft. Cronkhite   Sausalito, CA 94965

Shared Adventures

http://www.sharedadventures.org

A Santa Cruz, California based non-profit organization dedicated to bringing the outdoors into the lives of people with physical challenges and special needs. All photos were taken at the annual event, "Day on the Beach" where many volunteers see to it that people with disabilities share adventures in the ocean (such as surfing, kayaking, snorkeling...).

Endnotes

i. Brain Injury Association of America website (See Online References, Appendix F).
ii. Keyes, Ken Jr. *The Hundredth Monkey*, (1985).
iii. The title "The Virus" is an analogy. Brain injury is not an infectious disability.
iv. Psalm 23: 4-6
v. George Washington University, Special Education – Traumatic Brain Injury (See Appendix B and Online References).
vi. Moe T. Vator was a character developed for use in Heidi's research regarding the role of personal motivation in rehabilitation from brain injury - MOTIVATION/ REHABILITATION - Can adapting therapy to the student's interest make a difference? (See Gray Matters web page)
vii. "Peer Counselor" is dedicated to Christi Voenell of Central Coast Center for Independent Living - New Options project, Capitola, CA.
viii. I Chronicles, 4: 9-10
ix. Pilates, Joseph *Return to Life Through Controlology* (1998).
x. "Left and Right Hemisphere" uses information from Hannaford, Carla PhD, *Smart Moves – Why Learning is not all in your Head* (1995).
xi. Monterey Bay Aquarium webpage – Otter exhibit (see Online References)
xii. Trip report to Western Sea Kayakers
xiii. "Shared Adventure" is dedicated to Randy Carrillo. For Shared Adventures (program designed for promoting adventures for people with disabilities) see Online References.
xiv. L.A. Times, (October 5, 2004) On this day, San Onofre wave skiers/kayak surfers were taking paraplegics out in the surf on tandem rides. Heidi Lerner went surfing just to be out on the water with them. The media wound up taking her picture and used it in their article. Maybe It was her cute face :) or maybe they just caught her on a good ride!

Did you know that in California, in many locations, launching paddle-powered crafts is prohibited? Constraint on paddle powered crafts is a shame, as this limits surfers with disabilities who can only use a paddle craft. This prohibition restricts equal access in the surf!

[xv] Incapacitating, unbearable noise caused by military sonar and seismic air guns – used in oil and gas exploration, as well as increased background noise due to intensified shipping threatens marine mammals worldwide. Use of Low Frequency Active Sonar is being proposed by the U.S. Navy in increasing amounts (the U.S. is not the only country wanting to utilize high intensity sonar systems in their military) even though it is clearly shown to disrupt the web of life in the ocean and often has dire consequences for marine mammals, fish and other sea animals.
Did you know?
- One deployment of military sonar dangerously affects an area the size of Texas!
- Passive sonar systems exist that can be used to detect enemy submarines which do not cause violent, torturous acts to marine life.
- Use of LFAS and Seismic airguns can be routed to minimize the effects on marine mammals.

[xvi] For types of brain injury - (Closed, Open, Traumatic & Acquired) - see glossary.

[xvii] Iatrogenic – (see glossary).

[xviii] A touch of sarcasm

[xix] One final note to my readers: I have painted a picture of brain injury for the sake of your comprehension. Personally, due to time since my injury, academic interventions, psychosocial and emotional assistance I've gotten along the way, as well as persistence with personal development, I am no longer engulfed by most of the symptoms that I have talked about.